D0129713

1 CORINTHIANS

Taking on Tough Issues

Group Directory

Pass this Directory around and have your Group Members
fill in their names and phone numbers

Name   **Phone**

_____   _____

_____   _____

_____   _____

_____   _____

_____   _____

_____   _____

_____   _____

_____   _____

_____   _____

_____   _____

_____   _____

_____   _____

_____   _____

_____   _____

_____   _____

1 CORINTHIANS

Taking on Tough Issues

EDITING AND PRODUCTION TEAM:

James F. Couch, Jr., Lyman Coleman, Sharon Penington, Cathy Tardif,
Christopher Werner, Matthew Lockhart, Erika Tiepel, Richard Peace,
Andrew Sloan, Mike Shepherd, Keith Madsen,
Katharine Harris, Scott Lee

NASHVILLE, TENNESSEE

Taking on Tough Issues: A Study of Integrity Based on 1 Corinthians
© 1988, 1998, 2003 Serendipity House
Reprinted August 2004

Published by Serendipity House Publishers
Nashville, Tennessee

All rights reserved. No part of this work may be reproduced, stored in a retrieval system, or transmitted in any form or by any means, electronic or mechanical, including photo-copying and recording, without express written permission of the publisher. Requests for permission should be addressed to Serendipity House, 117 10th Avenue North, Nashville, TN 37234.

ISBN: 1-5749-4321-9

Dewey Decimal Classification: 227.2
Subject Headings:
BIBLE. N.T. 1 CORINTHIANS-STUDY AND TEACHING \ CHRISTIAN LIFE

Unless otherwise indicated, Scripture quotations are taken from the
Holman Christian Standard Bible®,
Copyright © 1999, 2000, 2002, 2003 by Holman Bible Publishers.
Used by permission.

To purchase additional copies of this resource or other studies:
ORDER ONLINE at www.SerendipityHouse.com
WRITE Serendipity House, 117 10th Avenue North, Nashville, TN 37234
FAX (615) 277-8181
PHONE (800) 525-9563

1-800-525-9563
www.SerendipityHouse.com

Printed in the United States of America
10 09 08 07 06 05 04   2 3 4 5 6 7 8 9 10

Table of Contents

Core Values

Community:
: The purpose of this curriculum is to build community within the body of believers around Jesus Christ.

Group Process:
: To build community, the curriculum must be designed to take a group through a step-by-step process of sharing your story with one another.

Interactive Bible Study:
: To share your "story," the approach to Scripture in the curriculum needs to be open-ended and right brain—to "level the playing field" and encourage everyone to share.

Developmental Stages:
: To provide a healthy program throughout the four stages of the life cycle of a group, the curriculum needs to offer courses on three levels of commitment: (1) Beginner Level—low-level entry, high structure, to level the playing field; (2) Growth Level—deeper Bible study, flexible structure, to encourage group accountability; (3) Discipleship Level—in-depth Bible study, open structure, to move the group into high gear.

Target Audiences:
: To build community throughout the culture of the church, the curriculum needs to be flexible, adaptable and transferable into the structure of the average church.

Mission:
: To expand the Kingdom of God one person at a time by filling the "empty chair." (We add an extra chair to each group session to remind us of our mission.)

Introduction

Each healthy small group will move through various stages as it matures.

Growth Stage: Here the group begins to care for one another as it learns to apply what they learn through Bible study, worship and prayer.

Develop Stage: The inductive Bible study deepens while the group members discover and develop gifts and skills. The group explores ways to invite their neighbors and coworkers to group meetings.

Birth Stage: This is the time in which group members form relationships and begin to develop community. The group will spend more time in ice-breaker exercises, relational Bible study and covenant building.

Multiply Stage: The group begins the multiplication process. Members pray about their involvement in new groups. The "new" groups begin the life cycle again with the Birth Stage.

Subgrouping: If you have nine or more people at a meeting, Serendipity recommends you divide into subgroups of 3–6 for the Bible study. Ask one person to be the leader of each subgroup and to follow the directions for the Bible study. After 30 minutes, the Group Leader will call "time" and ask all subgroups to come together for the Caring Time.

Each group meeting should include all parts of the "three-part agenda."

Ice-Breaker: Fun, history-giving questions are designed to warm the group and to build understanding about the other group members. You can choose to use all of the Ice-Breaker questions, especially if there is a new group member that will need help in feeling comfortable with the group.

Bible Study: The heart of each meeting is the reading and examination of the Bible. The questions are open, discover questions that lead to further inquiry. Reference notes are provided to give everyone a "level playing field." The emphasis is on understanding what the Bible says and applying the truth to real life. The questions for each session build. There is always at least one "going deeper" question provided. You should always leave time for the last of the "questions for interaction." Should you choose, you can use the optional "going deeper" question to satisfy the desire for the challenging questions in groups that have been together for a while.

Caring Time: All study should point us to actions. Each session ends with prayer and direction in caring for the needs of the group members. You can choose between several questions. You should always pray for the "empty chair." Who do you know that could fill that void in your group?

Sharing Your Story: These sessions are designed for members to share a little of their personal lives each time. Through a number of special techniques each member is encouraged to move from low risk, less personal sharing to higher risk responses. This helps develop the sense of community and facilitates caregiving.

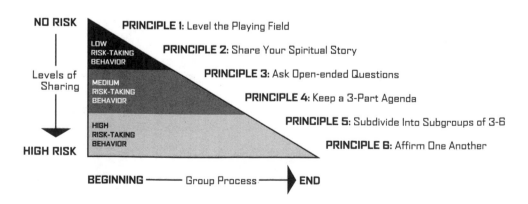

Group Covenant: A group covenant is a "contract" that spells out your expectations and the ground rules for your group. It's very important that your group discuss these issues—preferably as part of the first session.

GROUND RULES:

- Priority: While you are in the group, you give the group meeting priority.

- Participation: Everyone participates and no one dominates.

- Respect: Everyone is given the right to their own opinion and all questions are encouraged and respected.

- Confidentiality: Anything that is said in the meeting is never repeated outside the meeting.

- Empty Chair: The group stays open to new people at every meeting.

- Support: Permission is given to call upon each other in time of need—even in the middle of the night.

- Advice Giving: Unsolicited advice is not allowed.

- Mission: We agree to do everything in our power to start a new group as our mission.

ISSUES:

- The time and place this group is going to meet is_____

- Refreshments are _____ responsibility.

- Child care is _____ responsibility.

Divisions in the Church

Scripture 1 Corinthians 1:1–17

Corinth was an unusual city. After its capture by the Roman legions in 146 B.C., the city was leveled. It lay in waste for nearly 100 years until Julius Caesar rebuilt it in 44 B.C. Then it grew rapidly, thanks largely to its unique geographical location. Because it lay at the neck of a narrow isthmus connecting the two parts of Greece, it controlled all north-south land traffic. To the east and the west of the city were two fine harbors. Both goods and ships were hauled across the four-mile-wide Isthmus of Corinth. Thus Corinth also controlled most east-west sea routes. This strategic location commanded wealth and influence. By the time of Paul's visit some 100 years after its rebuilding, Corinth had become the capital of the province of Achaia and the third most important city in the Roman Empire, after Rome and Alexandria.

In this wealthy young city, excess seemed to be the norm, even in religion. The Greek author Pausanias describes 26 pagan shrines and temples, including the great temples of Apollo and Aphrodite. In Old Corinth, 1,000 temple prostitutes had served Aphrodite, the goddess of love, and New Corinth continued this tradition of sexual worship practices. The city developed a worldwide reputation for vice and debauchery. Not surprisingly, it was in Corinth that Paul had to fight a battle to prevent Christianity from succumbing to the debilitating enticements offered by paganism.

Luxury was the hallmark of Corinth. Because storms in the Aegean Sea were frequent and treacherous, sailors preferred to put into one of the harbors and transport their cargo to the other side by way of land—despite the exorbitant prices charged by the Corinthians. Consequently, goods from around the world passed through Corinthian ports, and some 400,000 slaves were kept in the city to provide labor for this arduous job.

Paul visited Corinth during his second missionary journey, probably in A.D. 50. Having been in some peril in Macedonia, he fled by ship to Athens (Acts 17:5–15). Not meeting with great success there (Acts 17:16–34), he then journeyed the short distance to Corinth, where he met Priscilla

Welcome to this study of 1 Corinthians! Together we will look at this important letter that has much to say about the unity of Christ's church and the gifts we bring to the work of that church. As we examine what Paul says to the Corinthian church, we will learn new things about our own gifts, how we can use them for the glory of God, and how God can bring us together as one with other believers.

and Aquila (Acts 18:1–3). At first he preached in the synagogue with success, but then the Jewish leadership forced him to leave, so he moved next door into the home of a Gentile. Hoping to silence him, the Jewish leadership eventually hauled Paul before the governor Gallio, but Gallio threw the case out of court as having no merit. After eighteen months (his longest stay anywhere except in Ephesus), Paul left and continued his missionary work in Syria.

Two events sparked the writing of 1 Corinthians some three or four years later. First, Paul heard that a divisive spirit was loose in the church (1:11). Second, he received a letter in which the Corinthians asked him questions about marriage and other matters (7:1). In addition, a delegation from Corinth completed his knowledge of the problem there (16:15–17). Being unable to visit personally, Paul sought to deal with the issues by letter. Thus, the Corinthian correspondence was begun.

The theme of 1 Corinthians is the unity of the church. That unity should be more important than personality issues (ch. 1), and is based on what Christ has done for the church (ch. 2–3). Immoral behavior and contentiousness can threaten that unity (ch. 5–7), as can insensitivity to each other's conscience (ch. 8–9) and self-focus while celebrating the Lord's Supper (ch. 11). On the other hand, using one's spiritual gifts, especially love, can build that unity (ch. 12–14).

The membership of the Corinthian church reflected the diverse and cosmopolitan nature of the city itself. There were some Jews in the congregation, but it was mainly Gentile. There were some wealthy people, but most were working class people, including slaves. This was not a group that probably would have been drawn together in the normal course of affairs, except for the fact that they had met Jesus and he had changed their lives. They didn't know a lot about Jesus yet, and when it came to lifestyle they certainly muddled Christianity and culture together. With God's grace, Paul's instruction and the Holy Spirit's power, they would learn, grow and find their unity.

 Ice-Breaker Connect With Your Group (15 minutes)

Today we are beginning our journey through 1 Corinthians with a look at the thankful heart that Paul has for his fellow believers, but also his concern for the divisions that are disrupting the fellowship. Take some time to get to know one another better by sharing your responses to the following questions.

1. When you were 8 years old, who was your hero? What about this person did you especially want to emulate?

2. Growing up, with whom did you quarrel the most? Over what?

3. What are you most thankful for about your church?

Leader

Be sure to read the introductory material in the front of this book prior to the first session. To help your group members get acquainted, have each person introduce him or herself and then take turns answering one or two of the Ice-Breaker questions. If time allows, you may want to discuss all three questions.

Bible Study Read Scripture and Discuss (30 minutes)

Leader
Select a member of the group ahead of time to read aloud the Scripture passage. Then discuss the Questions for Interaction, dividing into subgroups of three to six. Be sure to save time at the end for the Caring Time.

The Corinthian church was a gifted church. As we are about to read, Paul was amazed at how God had blessed this local body of believers. But carnality was also present, as we will discover throughout this book. Read 1 Corinthians 1:1–17 and note how division was hurting the church.

Divisions in the Church

1 Paul, called as an apostle of Christ Jesus by God's will, and our brother Sosthenes:

²To God's church at Corinth, to those who are sanctified in Christ Jesus and called as saints, with all those in every place who call on the name of Jesus Christ our Lord—theirs and ours.

³Grace to you and peace from God our Father and the Lord Jesus Christ.

⁴I always thank my God for you because of God's grace given to you in Christ Jesus, ⁵that by Him you were made rich in everything—in all speaking and all knowledge— ⁶as the testimony about Christ was confirmed among you, ⁷so that you do not lack any spiritual gift as you eagerly wait for the revelation of our Lord Jesus Christ. ⁸He will also confirm you to the end, blameless in the day of our Lord Jesus Christ. ⁹God is faithful; by Him you were called into fellowship with His Son, Jesus Christ our Lord.

¹⁰Now I urge you, brothers, in the name of our Lord Jesus Christ, that you all say the same thing, that there be no divisions among you, and that you be united with the same understanding and the same conviction. ¹¹For it has been reported to me about you, my brothers, by members of Chloe's household, that there are quarrels among you. ¹²What I am saying is this: each of you says, "I'm with Paul," or "I'm with Apollos," or "I'm with Cephas," or "I'm with Christ." ¹³Is Christ divided? Was it Paul who was crucified for you? Or were you baptized in Paul's name? ¹⁴I thank God that I baptized none of you except Crispus and Gaius, ¹⁵so that no one can say you had been baptized in my name. ¹⁶I did, in fact, baptize the household of Stephanas; beyond that, I don't know if I baptized anyone else. ¹⁷For Christ did not send me to baptize, but to preach the gospel—not with clever words, so that the cross of Christ will not be emptied of its effect.

1 Corinthians 1:1–17

Questions for Interaction

Leader
Refer to the Summary and Study Notes at the end of this session as needed. If 30 minutes is not enough time to answer all of the questions in this section, conclude the Bible Study by answering questions 6 and 7.

1. If you were to write a letter to someone right now to tell this person that you thank God for him or her, to whom would you write? What would you thank God for about this person?

2. When there are divisions or quarrels between you and a friend or family member, what is most frequently at the heart of the quarrel?

   ○ Money.
   ○ Control issues.
   ○ Political differences.
   ○ Theological differences.
   ○ The priority the friendship or relationship should have.
   ○ Other _____.

3. What was Paul particularly thankful for in the Corinthians?

4. What was causing the quarrels among the Corinthians (see notes on v. 12)? How big of an issue has this been in your own church?

5. Why are cliques and divisions causing so much damage in the church?

6. When, if ever, have you felt like you were not part of the "accepted group" in a church or Christian fellowship? What happened that caused you to feel that way, and what did you do about it?

7. If Paul were to write to you today, asking you to do one thing to help heal a division between you and someone else, what do you think he would tell you to do?

Going Deeper   If your group has time and/or wants a challenge, go on to this question.

8. Paul urges the Corinthians to "be united with the same understanding and the same conviction" (v. 10). Where is it essential that Christians agree in this way, and where might different viewpoints be acceptable and even healthy?

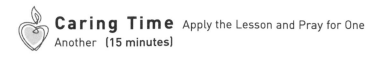 **Caring Time** Apply the Lesson and Pray for One Another (15 minutes)

This very important time is for expressing your concern for each other and to praying for one another.

Leader
Take some extra time in this first session to go over the introductory material at the front of this book. At the close, pass around your books and have everyone sign the Group Directory, also found in the front of this book.

1. Agree on the group covenant and ground rules that are described in the introduction to this book.

2. Pray about any divisions in your own church? (If your church has no such divisions, thank God for that.)

3. Share any other prayer requests and praises, and then close in prayer. Pray specifically for God to bring someone into your life next week to fill the empty chair.

NEXT WEEK *Today we looked at the causes behind the divisions in the Corinthian church, and how these divisions are like our own experience. In the coming week, follow through on your answer to question 7, and help to bring healing to a division in your own life or the life of your church. Next week we will consider the nature of Christian wisdom and how it compares to the "wisdom" of the world.*

Summary: He must face some very difficult issues in this letter. But rather than plunging right in with a spirit of judgment and a list of rules, he begins with thanksgiving. Whatever irregularities might exist at Corinth, they do so in the context of the good work that God has done in their midst.

The first problem that Paul deals with is divisions within the church. It seems that the Corinthians had begun to view Christianity as a new philosophy ("wisdom"), and the apostles were regarded (and judged) as if they were itinerant philosophers. He points out that Christian teachers are all servants of the same God, not philosophers competing with one another for an audience (3:5–4:21).

1:1 *an apostle.* Paul does not always identify himself by this title (e.g., 1 Thess. 1:1). He may do so here because his authority as an apostle is an issue with the Corinthians. An apostle is "one who is sent," "an envoy." It is an office held by those who witnessed the resurrected Christ and were called by Christ to this position. Their special job was to plant new churches throughout the Roman Empire. ***by God's will.*** Paul did not just decide that he would like to be an apostle and then proclaim himself one. God made it quite clear that he had chosen Paul for this task (Acts 22:21). ***our brother.*** Sosthenes is not an apostle. He is, however, a child of God the Father and thus part of God's family (as are all Christians). That is the basis on which Christians are meant to relate to one another—as kin, with sharing, care and patient love. ***Sosthenes.*** It is possible that this is the same Sosthenes from Acts 18:17.

1:2 *sanctified.* Consecrated, dedicated to the service of God. ***called.*** In the same way that Paul was called to be an apostle (v. 1), every believer is called by God to be holy. ***as saints.*** This refers to persons who are set apart to serve God's purposes, in much the same fashion as in the Old Testament where priests were set apart to serve a special religious function. In the New Testament all believers are "saints" (i.e., holy persons).

1:3 *Grace to you and peace.* Grace is the unmerited gift of God by which a person comes into sal-

vation. Peace is the outcome of that salvation, and has the idea of "wholeness" and "health."

1:5 *in everything.* Gifts of grace include salvation itself (v. 2), special supernatural gifts (v. 5), and acquittal on the Day of Judgment (v. 8). ***in all speaking.*** This is probably a reference to the gift of tongues (12:10), to prophecy (14:1) and to messages of wisdom and knowledge (12:8). In Corinth, the oratory of philosophers was common and valued. As part of their riches in Christ, the Christians too, it seems, had been given various speech-related abilities. This, however, led to problems in the church that Paul deals with in this letter. ***knowledge.*** The ability to understand and apply Christian truth.

1:7 *you do not lack any spiritual gift.* This is said both seriously (since Christians have at their disposal all of God's grace-gifts) and tongue-in-cheek (as Paul echoes their own boasting). ***spiritual gift.*** *Charismata,* Paul's word for the special gifts given by God, such as the gift of healing or of speaking in tongues. These gifts had a special fascination for the Corinthians. They serve as direct witnesses to the supernatural nature of Christianity.

1:8 *blameless.* Christians need not fear judgment since Jesus himself has already secured their acquittal by his death.

1:10 *I urge you.* "I beg you, I beseech you." This matter of their divisions is serious and must be dealt with. ***brothers.*** This is the basis of his appeal. Paul can write this way because they are all related to one another. It is not merely a matter of belonging to the same organization. They are part of the same family. ***all say the same thing.*** This does not mean that we become clones of each other. It means that we agree about what is at the heart of the matter: the lordship of Jesus Christ. ***divisions.*** *Schismata* (from which the English word "schisms" comes); a word often used to describe tears in a piece of clothing. ***united with the same understanding and the same conviction.*** Their disunity is rooted in differing ideas (doctrines). To be restored, to knit back together the church which is torn apart, requires a unity of understanding.

1:12 Various Christian leaders unwittingly have become rallying points for dissension. ***I'm with Paul.*** Paul does not commend those "on his side." A faction in his name is no better than any other faction. In fact, these people had probably exaggerated and falsified his actual viewpoints. ***I'm with Apollos.*** After Priscilla and Aquila had instructed him in the Gospel, Apollos went to Corinth to assist the church there. ***I'm with Cephas.*** Cephas is the Jewish form of the name Peter. It is probable that Peter also visited Corinth. ***I'm with Christ.*** These are possibly the people who look with disdain on the other groups who profess allegiance to the Christ preached by Paul, by Apollos or by Cephas. Instead, they profess allegiance to the Christ they know without the teaching of anyone.

1:17 Here Paul comes to the principle that is at the root of the problem in Corinth. They can form such factions only because they misunderstand the nature of God's wisdom. ***clever words.*** This is *Sophia,* a word often translated as "wisdom" and a key word in this letter. Paul uses it in both positive and negative ways. Here the idea is negative. This is wisdom defined as the skillful use of human reason with a view to convincing the hearer of the truth of a position. ***the cross of Christ will not be emptied.*** Paul is eager that people be persuaded by Christ crucified and not by mere eloquence.

True Wisdom

Scripture 1 Corinthians 1:18–2:5

LAST WEEK *In last week's session, we looked at the division that was hurting the Corinthian church. We were reminded of how important it is that each of us work on maintaining unity in our church and in our personal lives. Today we will look at what true wisdom is, where it comes from and how we can use that wisdom in our lives.*

Ice-Breaker Connect With Your Group (15 minutes)

Leader
Begin the session with a word of prayer. Have your group members take turns sharing their responses to one, two or all three of the Ice-Breaker questions. Be sure that everyone gets a chance to participate.

When we think of wisdom, we may be reminded of the story of King Solomon, who asked for wisdom above all else when the Lord God said he would grant anything he desired. The Lord was so pleased with his request that he also gave him riches and power. Take turns sharing your thoughts and experiences concerning seeking wisdom.

1. When you were a teenager, who were you most likely to go to for wisdom?

   ○ My parents or another relative.
   ○ An advice columnist, like Ann Landers or Dear Abby.
   ○ One of my friends.
   ○ A teacher.
   ○ Other _____.

2. When you were younger, who were you most likely to "debate" about an issue?

   ○ My parents.
   ○ My siblings or friends.
   ○ My teachers.
   ○ Opponents on an actual debate team.
   ○ No one—I was docile and agreed.

3. What would you nominate as the most stirring and wise?

⭘ Martin Luther King's "I Have a Dream" speech.
⭘ Lincoln's Gettysburg Address.
⭘ Kennedy's "I Am a Berliner" speech.
⭘ FDR's "We Have Nothing to Fear, but Fear Itself" address.
⭘ Other _____.

Bible Study Read Scripture and Discuss (30 minutes)

Christians are sometimes mocked as not being too bright. It is said that we "follow our faith blindly." Yet, as we are about to read, we follow a God who has all wisdom and shares it with us so that we may boast in him and not ourselves. Read 1 Corinthians 1:18–2:5 and note how God's wisdom is worth far more than gold or riches.

Leader
Select two members of the group ahead of time to read aloud the Scripture passage. Have one member read 1:18–25, and the other read 1:26–2:5. Then discuss the Questions for Interaction, dividing into subgroups of three to six.

True Wisdom

Reader One: ¹⁸For to those who are perishing the message of the cross is foolishness, but to us who are being saved it is God's power. ¹⁹For it is written:

> I will destroy the wisdom of the wise,
> and I will set aside the understanding of the experts.

²⁰Where is the philosopher? Where is the scholar? Where is the debater of this age? Hasn't God made the world's wisdom foolish? ²¹For since, in God's wisdom, the world did not know God through wisdom, God was pleased to save those who believe through the foolishness of the message preached. ²²For the Jews ask for signs and the Greeks seek wisdom, ²³but we preach Christ crucified, a stumbling block to the Jews and foolishness to the Gentiles. ²⁴Yet to those who are called, both Jews and Greeks, Christ is God's power and God's wisdom, ²⁵because God's foolishness is wiser than human wisdom, and God's weakness is stronger than human strength.

Reader Two: ²⁶Brothers, consider your calling: not many are wise from a human perspective, not many powerful, not many of noble birth. ²⁷Instead, God has chosen the world's foolish things to shame the wise, and God has chosen the world's weak things to shame the strong. ²⁸God has chosen the world's insignificant and despised things—the things viewed as nothing—so He might bring to nothing the things that are viewed as some-thing, ²⁹so that no one can boast in His presence. ³⁰But from Him you are in Christ Jesus, who for us became wisdom from God, as well as righteousness, sanctification, and redemption, ³¹in order that, as it is written: "The one who boasts must boast in the Lord."

2When I came to you, brothers, announcing the testimony of God to you, I did not come with brilliance of speech or wisdom. ²For I determined to know nothing among you except Jesus Christ and Him crucified. ³And I was with you in weakness, in fear, and in much trembling. ⁴My speech and my proclamation were not with persuasive words of wisdom, but with a demonstration of the Spirit and power, ⁵so that your faith might not be based on men's wisdom but on God's power.

1 Corinthians 1:18–2:5

Questions for Interaction

Leader
Refer to the Summary and Study Notes at the end of this session as needed. If 30 minutes is not enough time to answer all of the questions in this section, conclude the Bible Study by answering questions 6 and 7.

1. When you do something foolish, in which of the following ways are you most likely to react?

   ○ Act like it was what I meant to do.
   ○ Laugh at myself.
   ○ Get angry and defensive.
   ○ Brush myself off and move on.
   ○ Get angry at myself and call myself names under my breath.
   ○ Other _____.

2. What had some of the people of Paul's time thought of as foolishness? What did they think was foolish about it?

3. Paul said, "the world did not know God through wisdom" (1:21). Do you agree that worldly wisdom or philosophy alone is insufficient to know what God is like? Why or why not?

4. Why did God choose the foolish, weak and insignificant things of the world (1:27–28)? In what ways have you seen God use these types of people?

5. What was the central focus of Paul's message (2:2)? Why might philosophical speculations dilute that message?

6. When have you felt like you were "insignificant and despised" (1:28)? How did God use you at that time of your life?

7. What could you "boast" about that the Lord has done in and through you (1:31)?

Going Deeper   If your group has time and/or wants a challenge, go on to this question.

8. Should we view what Paul says in this passage as a discouragement of pursuing fields of human learning? Why or why not? Are there ways in which our studies and research can help illuminate the wisdom of God for those who are having difficulty understanding it?

Caring Time Apply the Lesson and Pray for One Another (15 minutes)

Gather around each other now and support one another in a time of sharing and prayer. Remember that God is the source of all wisdom and he has given you the Holy Spirit to help you pray according to his will.

Leader
Bring the group back together and begin the Caring Time by sharing responses to all three questions. Then take turns sharing prayer requests and having a time of group prayer. Be sure to include prayer for the empty chair.

1. How would you describe this past week for you? Why?

   ○ Everything was smooth.
   ○ It seemed that I was running up hill all week.
   ○ My week was up and down, up and down.
   ○ The week started slow, but it finished great.
   ○ Things started great, but I got bogged down later in the week.
   ○ This week was a snooze.
   ○ Other _____.

2. Take time to thank God for the things he has done in and through you, as you shared in answer to question 7.

3. What situations are you facing in this coming week that you will need divine wisdom to handle?

   P.S. *Add new group members to the Group Directory at the front of this book.*

NEXT WEEK *Today we considered the nature of Christian wisdom and how it compares to the "wisdom" of the world. We were reminded that we are able to accomplish anything if we rely on the power and wisdom of God. In the coming week, step out of your comfort zone and talk to someone about what Christ has done in your life. Next week we will discuss how Christ must remain the one foundation of the church for it to have power.*

Summary: The fact that the Corinthians can boast of party slogans is a clear indication that they over-value human wisdom and misunderstand the nature of the Gospel. Paul shows that the Gospel is decidedly not a species of human philosophy, because it involves such a reversal of human expectation. Who would have thought that God would work through the scandal of the cross? Only God could demonstrate his power through a dying, powerless "criminal." Paul then goes on to "prove" that God does indeed work through weakness. He first looks at the Corinthians (1:26–31) and then at himself (2:1–5). He points out that they were not very clever and he was not very persuasive. So the fact they are Christians proves that God works through weakness. How else could the fact of the church at Corinth be explained?

1:18 *perishing.* Unless they repent (turn around and go the other way), they will not be acquitted on the Day of Judgment. ***the message of the cross.*** This is the only legitimate slogan. Paul puts the issue in stark terms: the question of eternal destiny centers on the meaning of the Cross. Their misunderstanding and division is no slight matter. It strikes at the core of the Gospel. ***foolishness.*** It is absurd to many that God's redemptive activity involves death by crucifixion. ***being saved.*** Salvation is a process, begun at conversion, consummated at the Second Coming, and fulfilled in the New Age.

1:19 Paul quotes Isaiah 29:14 to demonstrate that human-centered wisdom will be overthrown by God.

1:20 All those who represent human wisdom are forced to flee in the face of God's revelation that their wisdom is actually mere folly.

1:22 *Jews ask for signs.* The Jews expected a Messiah who would come in obvious power doing miraculous deeds. In Jesus they saw one so weak that his enemies were able to kill him. ***Greeks seek wisdom.*** Their delight was in clever, cunning logic delivered with soaring persuasiveness. That a Jewish peasant who died as a convicted criminal could be the focus of God's redemptive plan was so silly to them as to be laughable.

1:23 *stumbling block.* Literally, "a scandal." Jesus' crucifixion "proved" to the Jews that he could not be of God (Deut. 21:23, those hanging from a tree are cursed of God). A suffering, dying Messiah was totally outside first-century Jewish expectations. ***foolishness.*** Both the Incarnation and Crucifixion were actions Greeks felt were unworthy of their gods. The cradle and the cross show that people cannot reach God through the route of power, wisdom or reason, but only by the response of faith to that which has been done for them.

1:26 *consider your calling.* In their own calling they see the paradox of the all-powerful God using the "weak things of the world." ***wise.*** This refers to people with education or philosophical training. ***powerful.*** This means people in high positions politically or socially. ***noble birth.*** These were people of distinguished families who may have held Roman citizenship.

1:27 *the world's foolish things.* Those who in the estimation of the current culture were insignificant. ***to shame.*** The calling of the insignificant shows that the opinions of the "wise" about the worth of certain people or about how one approached God were wrong.

1:28 *the things viewed as nothing/the things that are viewed as something.* God chooses the "nobodies" and thus exposes the foolishness of the way the world defines the "somebodies."

1:30 *But from Him.* They owe their relationship to God solely to Jesus Christ. ***wisdom from God.*** Paul spoke of "human wisdom" in 1:17, i.e., philosophical wisdom. Here he begins to "de-philosophize" *sophia* (wisdom) and instead historicize it. The historical Jesus is God's wisdom. It is Christ who mediates God's plan of salvation. ***righteousness.*** Christ is their righteousness in that he took upon himself the guilt of human sin. So on the Last Day when Christians stand before the Judge, they are viewed not in terms of their own failure and inadequacy but as being "in Christ." ***sanctification.*** Human beings cannot come before a Holy God because they are not holy; but once again, Christ provides what people lack. His holiness sanctifies them and a relationship with God is assured. ***redemption.*** It is by Christ's redeeming work on the cross that wisdom, righteousness and holiness are mediated to humankind.

1:31 Here Paul quotes Jeremiah 9:24.

2:2 In Corinth, a city teeming with articulate philosophers, Paul's refusal to make persuasive speech and brilliant logic preeminent in his evangelism was especially striking. Instead, he simply told of the crucified Christ, "the most scandalous feature of the Christian message." Some scholars believe he took this approach because he had recently been in Athens, where a more philosophical approach brought minimal results (Acts 17:16–34).

2:3 This weakness and fear was not for his safety, but due to Paul's sense of the awesome responsibility he had as a preacher of the Gospel (2 Cor. 2:16).

2:4 Paul says he was not an impressive speaker (2 Cor. 10:1), even though his writing (which often has the "feel" of speech) is frequently quite eloquent. ***a demonstration of the Spirit and power.*** Paul reveals the secret behind the impact that his preaching made. People were moved by the convicting power of the Holy Spirit. This is the real proof of the validity of the Gospel.

One Foundation

Scripture 1 Corinthians 3:1–17

> **LAST WEEK** *The nature of God's wisdom and how it compares to the "wisdom" of the world was our topic in last week's session. We were reminded that true wisdom comes from God and that he works through us to accomplish his will on this earth. Therefore, we can only boast in the Lord, and not in ourselves. This week we will consider the need to build the church on the one secure foundation of Jesus Christ.*

Ice-Breaker Connect With Your Group (15 minutes)

Very often we don't even think about the stability of our homes or other buildings until an earthquake or storm hits. Then we start hoping the architect and builder laid a strong foundation with safety in mind. Take turns sharing your unique experiences with building things.

1. Which of the following did you most enjoy building when you were a child, and who helped you?

   ○ A fort.
   ○ A snowman or igloo.
   ○ A tree house.
   ○ A Popsicle stick house.
   ○ A soapbox derby racer.
   ○ Other _____.

Leader
Choose one or two Ice-Breaker questions. If you have someone new in your group you may want to do all three to help the new member get acquainted. Remember to stick closely to the three-part agenda and the time allowed for each segment.

2. What have you been most involved in building as an adult?

- ○ A house.
- ○ Debt.
- ○ My reputation.
- ○ A secure future.
- ○ A business.
- ○ Things for my kids.
- ○ Other _____.

3. On a scale of 1 ("Don't huff or puff or it will all fall down!") to 10 ("I could have my own tool show"), how would you rate yourself as a builder of things?

 Bible Study Read Scripture and Discuss (30 minutes)

Each one of us who follows Christ has a role in his kingdom. As Paul writes, it is important for us to do our part and feel valued in it. But it is all in vain if our core values for what we do as a church are not built on the foundation of Jesus Christ, who he is and what his purpose is for us. Read 1 Corinthians 3:1–17 and note the responsibility we have in being God's sanctuary.

Leader
Select a member of the group ahead of time to read aloud the Scripture passage. Then discuss the Questions for Interaction, dividing into subgroups of three to six.

One Foundation

3 Brothers, I was not able to speak to you as spiritual people but as people of the flesh, as babies in Christ. [2]I fed you milk, not solid food, because you were not yet able to receive it. In fact, you are still not able, [3]because you are still fleshly. For since there is envy and strife among you, are you not fleshly and living like ordinary people? [4]For whenever someone says, "I'm with Paul," and another, "I'm with Apollos," are you not typical men?

[5]So, what is Apollos? And what is Paul? They are servants through whom you believed, and each has the role the Lord has given. [6]I planted, Apollos watered, but God gave the growth. [7]So then neither the one who plants nor the one who waters is anything, but only God who gives the growth. [8]Now the one who plants and the one who waters are equal, and each will receive his own reward according to his own labor. [9]For we are God's co-workers. You are God's field, God's building. [10]According to God's grace that was given to me, as a skilled master builder I have laid a foundation, and another builds on it. But each one must be careful how he builds on it, [11]because no one can lay any other foundation than what has been laid—that is, Jesus Christ. [12]If anyone builds on the foundation with gold, silver, costly stones, wood, hay, or straw, [13]each one's work will become obvious, for the day will disclose it, because it will be revealed by fire; the fire will test the quality of each one's work. [14]If anyone's work that he has built survives, he will receive a reward. [15]If anyone's work is burned up, it will be lost, but he will be saved; yet it will be like an escape through fire.

[16]Don't you know that you are God's sanctuary and that the Spirit of God lives in you? [17]If anyone ruins God's sanctuary, God will ruin him; for God's sanctuary is holy, and that is what you are.

1 Corinthians 3:1–17

Questions for Interaction

Leader
Refer to the Summary and Study Notes at the end of this session as needed. If 30 minutes is not enough time to answer all of the questions in this section, conclude the Bible Study by answering question 7.

1. If Paul was your "spiritual nutritionist" at this point in your life, which of the following diets would he be most likely to put you on?

    ○ Pure "milk"—I'm still in the infant stage.
    ○ Maybe milk with a little of that baby cereal—I'm beginning to grow a little.
    ○ A steady diet of "happy meals"—I need positive input.
    ○ A varied diet including milk—I need something to chew on, but I can't forget the basics.
    ○ Where's the beef?

2. What needs to happen before one is able to receive "solid food" spiritually (see vv. 1–3 and notes on those verses)? What signs might you look for in yourself or one you are mentoring?

3. From verses 6–9, who plants? Who waters? Who is the field? Who is responsible for growth? How does this illustration relate to the problem in the Corinthian church?

4. What is the sole foundation for all Christian building? What other false "foundations" might one try?

5. What is Paul saying in verses 12–15 about our individual contributions to building God's kingdom?

6. Who are the people God has used in your own life—the "Paul" who planted and the "Apollos" who watered? In whose lives have you planted and/or watered?

7. On a scale of 1 (straw) to 10 (gold), how sturdy is your spiritual "building"? How does that compare to one year ago? What are you doing to grow as a Christian? What do you need to do?

8. In what ways are you seeing people within the church destroying God's temple through what they are doing? What can people in this group do to counteract such destruction?

Caring Time Apply the Lesson and Pray for One Another **(15 minutes)**

Encouraging and supporting each other is especially vital if this group is to become all it can be. Take time now to build up one another with sharing and prayer.

Leader
Begin the Caring Time by having group members respond to all three questions. Be sure to save at least the last five minutes for a time of group prayer. Remember to include a prayer for the empty chair when concluding the prayer time.

1. What is the best thing that happened to you last week? What is the worst?

2. Pray for the people that God has called you to "plant" or "water." Could you invite one of those people to fill the empty chair next week?

3. How can the group pray for you as you seek to grow as a Christian and build your faith, as you shared about in question 7?

NEXT WEEK *Today we discussed how Christ is to be the foundation of the church. We were reminded that we must be careful how we build on our foundation of Jesus Christ, because we are "God's sanctuary." In the coming week, "water" those around you with love and prayer. Next week we will look at some "power games" that were played in the Corinthian church, at Paul's expense, and how he dealt with such power games.*

Summary: Paul returns to the question of factions in the Corinthian church. The problem is that by misunderstanding the nature of wisdom and then exalting certain teachers, they reveal their immaturity as Christians. Instead, the Corinthian Christians need to understand that they are God's field and God's building; and that Paul, Apollos and the others are mere servants who assist God in bringing about their growth. By pretending to be "wise" (by the standards of the world), they show themselves to be "foolish" (in the eyes of God). They must stop exalting men, put an end to their divisions and rest in the fact that "all things" are already theirs.

3:1 *Brothers.* Despite his criticism they are still part of the same family. The issue is not whether they are true Christians or not, but whether they are mature or immature in their faith. ***spiritual.*** A mature Christian whose life is dominated by the indwelling Spirit. ***people of the flesh.*** Those Christians who are molded more by the spirit of the age than by the Spirit of God; whose life and thoughts are so immature that they are "babies in Christ."

3:2 I fed you milk. Paul continues his metaphor. When he was in Corinth, they were not yet ready for "solid food." ***were not yet able.*** To his disappointment, they are still immature.

3:3 Jealousy and quarreling are clear indications that the Spirit does not control their lives and that they are still "babies." ***ordinary people.*** Their lifestyle is not in accord with that of the mature Christian. By exalting certain teachers, they betray their lack of understanding of the Gospel. Paul's point is that although they have the Spirit, they are acting precisely like people without the Spirit. In fact, given the emphasis in chapters 12–14, they thought rather highly of their own spirituality.

3:5 *servants.* Paul and Apollos are not to be exalted. They are merely servants and not of very high order. This same word is used to describe a waiter. They were just carrying out the task God for which had called them.

3:6 *I planted.* Paul was the first to preach in Corinth. ***Apollos watered.*** Apollos continued Paul's work by helping to build up a new church. ***God gave the growth.*** Their labors alone would not have been enough. The growth came from God.

3:8 *are equal.* Paul and Apollos were colleagues, not rivals. They had the same ultimate purpose, even though they had different specific tasks to fulfill (one began the work, the other nurtured it).

3:9 *God's field.* The Corinthians are the field that God is plowing through his servants. God's building. Paul's analogy shifts from agriculture to architecture.

3:10 *master.* Literally, "wise." Paul continues to develop the idea of wisdom. ***builder.*** (In Greek, *architekton.*) The one who plans and supervises the construction of a building, not the one who does the actual labor. ***I have laid a foundation.*** By preaching Christ, who is the foundation (v. 11), Paul was the one who began the work in Corinth (v. 6).

3:11 A community might be built on another foundation, but it would not be the church. The church's only foundation is Jesus Christ (1:18–25).

3:12 Paul describes some of the ways a person can go astray in building on the foundation—namely by using inferior or inadequate materials. ***gold, silver, costly stones.*** These materials will survive the test of fire. ***wood, hay, or straw.*** These will burn up.

3:13 *the day.* On the Day of Judgment the quality of labor will be revealed. ***revealed by fire.*** The idea is not of fire as punishment, but as a means of testing—a way of revealing the "the quality of each one's work." This is a strong warning to those who lead the church.

3:16 *sanctuary.* Paul tells them what kind of building they as a community are becoming (the reference is not to individual believers, but to the corporate body). This would be a particularly vivid and exciting image for the Corinthians, surrounded as they were by pagan temples, because Paul shows them that within their community—wherever it gathered—God's Spirit was at work creating a new people.

3:17 *ruins.* The idea has shifted from losing one's pay for having used inferior building materials (vv. 12–15) to being punished for destroying the church. If the Corinthians continue to quarrel, instead of accepting the leadership of God's Spirit, they defile God's holy temple and will be marked for destruction.

Power Plays

Scripture 1 Corinthians 4:1–21

LAST WEEK *Last week we talked about the need to build the church on the secure foundation of Jesus Christ. We were reminded that one day the quality of our faith will be tested, so we need to carefully choose the building materials we use to construct "God's sanctuary" (3:16–17). This week we will gain some understanding about the "power plays" that were being used in the Corinthian church, how Paul dealt with them and what his actions say for the church today.*

 Ice-Breaker Connect With Your Group (15 minutes)

Many of us are overwhelmed with responsibilities and "to do lists." We even need computers and huge day-planners to make sure we live up to all of our commitments. Take turns sharing your experiences about fulfilling your responsibilities.

Leader
Welcome and introduce new group members. Choose one, two or all three of the Ice-Breaker questions.

1. Which of the following responsibilities or chores were you entrusted with when you were a teenager? Which did you like the most? Which did you like the least?

   ○ Caring for younger siblings.
   ○ Doing yard work.
   ○ Cleaning my room.
   ○ Helping with house cleaning.
   ○ Doing the dishes.
   ○ Farm chores.
   ○ Helping prepare meals.
   ○ Taking out the trash.
   ○ Ironing or mending clothes.
   ○ Other _____.

2. When it came to doing what you were entrusted with as a teenager, how faithful were you? On a scale of 1 ("You could rely on me NOT doing it!") to 10 ("Once asked, it was as good as done!"), how would you rate yourself?

3. What do you consider to be the most important thing you are entrusted with right now?

 Bible Study Read Scripture and Discuss (30 minutes)

Leader
Select three members of the group ahead of time to read aloud the Scripture passage. Have one member read verses 1–5; another read verses 6–13; and the third person read verses 14–21. Then discuss the Questions for Interaction, dividing into subgroups of three to six.

Arrogance is a sin that can destroy the influence of Christ in a family, community and church. Here Paul rebukes the church in Corinth for getting caught up in making Christianity about them and not about the kingdom. Read 1 Corinthians 4:1–21 and note how Paul turns them back to Christ and the Gospel.

Power Plays

Reader One: 4 A person should consider us in this way: as servants of Christ and managers of God's mysteries. [2]In this regard, it is expected of managers that each one be found faithful. [3]It is of little importance that I should be evaluated by you or by a human court. In fact, I don't even evaluate myself. [4]For I am not conscious of anything against myself, but I am not justified by this. The One who evaluates me is the Lord. [5]Therefore don't judge anything prematurely, before the Lord comes, who will both bring to light what is hidden in darkness and reveal the intentions of the hearts. And then praise will come to each one from God.

Reader Two: [6]Now, brothers, I have applied these things to myself and Apollos for your benefit, so that you may learn from us the saying: "Nothing beyond what is written." The purpose is that none of you will be inflated with pride in favor of one person over another. [7]For who makes you so superior? What do you have that you didn't receive? If, in fact, you did receive it, why do you boast as if you hadn't received it? [8]Already you are full! Already you are rich! You have begun to reign as kings without us—and I wish you did reign, so that we also could reign with you! [9]For I think God has displayed us, the apostles, in last place, like men condemned to die: we have become a spectacle to the world and to angels and to men. [10]We are fools for Christ, but you are wise in Christ! We are weak, but you are strong! You are distinguished, but we are dishonored! [11]Up to the present hour we are both hungry and thirsty; we are poorly clothed, roughly treated, homeless; [12]we labor, working with our own hands. When we are reviled, we bless; when we are persecuted, we endure it; [13]when we are slandered, we entreat. We are, even now, like the world's garbage, like the filth of all things.

Reader Three: ¹⁴I'm not writing this to shame you, but to warn you as my dear children. ¹⁵For you can have 10,000 instructors in Christ, but you can't have many fathers. Now I have fathered you in Christ Jesus through the gospel. ¹⁶Therefore I urge you, be imitators of me. ¹⁷This is why I have sent to you Timothy, who is my beloved and faithful child in the Lord. He will remind you about my ways in Christ Jesus, just as I teach every-where in every church. ¹⁸Now some are inflated with pride, as though I were not coming to you. ¹⁹But I will come to you soon, if the Lord wills, and I will know not the talk but the power of those who are inflated with pride. ²⁰For the kingdom of God is not in talk but in power. ²¹What do you want? Should I come to you with a rod, or in love and a spirit of gentleness?

1 Corinthians 4:1–21

Questions for Interaction

Leader
Refer to the Summary and Study Notes at the end of this session as needed. If 30 minutes is not enough time to answer all of the questions in this section, conclude the Bible Study by answering questions 6 and 7.

1. When you feel like people are judging or evaluating you, how are you most likely to react?

   ○ By defending myself.
   ○ By getting away from them as quickly as possible.
   ○ By finding some things to criticize about them.
   ○ By listening to what they say with an open mind.
   ○ By immediately trying to become what they want me to become.
   ○ Other _____.

2. How does Paul respond to the perception that some in the Corinthian church seem to be judging or evaluating him? What do you learn about Paul from the way that he handles this?

3. What application does verse 7 have for people who are being arrogant or boastful?

4. In light of what Paul has previously said (1:18–2:5), what is significant about Paul's use of the words "fools" and "weak" (v. 10) to describe himself and others?

5. How is Paul countering the moves some are making to attain power and authority over the Corinthian church?

6. Where are you seeking power in your life right now? Are you seeking this power through your own natural ability like some of the Corinthians, or through God as Paul sought to do? How are you using the power you have?

7. Reflecting honestly on verse 20, do you feel your Christian life is a matter of talk or more of power? What can you do to "walk the talk" this week?

8. When dealing with church conflict, how do you know when to approach with "a rod" and when to approach "in love and a spirit of gentleness"?

 Caring Time Apply the Lesson and Pray for One
Another **(15 minutes)**

Leader
Be sure to save at least 15 minutes for this important time. After sharing responses to all three questions and asking for prayer requests, close in a time of group prayer.

Once again, take some time now to encourage one another in your faith by discussing the following questions and sharing prayer requests.

1. Where are you in the journey of following Christ?

   ○ I am a seeker.
   ○ I have just begun the journey.
   ○ I'm returning after getting lost on the wrong path.
   ○ I've been following Christ for a long time.
   ○ Other _____.

2. How do you need God's help in the coming week to help you "walk the talk" and follow through on your answer to question 7?

3. What conflicts are you having with people who are "inflated with pride" and feel "superior" (vv. 6–7)? Pray for insight on how to handle those conflicts.

NEXT WEEK *Today we focused on a conflict that Paul was having with some people in the Corinthian church who thought they were superior to others. We were reminded that we should not trust in our own abilities, but rather in God's power and strength. In the coming week, ask the Holy Spirit to open your eyes to the sin of pride in your life and pray to always rely on God as your source of power. Next week we will look at some warnings Paul gave the Corinthians on sexual immorality.*

Summary: Paul must reassert his authority as an apostle over the church (so he can deal with the problems there). He must do so without negating what he has said about the value of the work of other leaders like Apollos. In chapter 4, he asserts his special authority by reminding them of the role he played in their spiritual life. He is their spiritual father.

4:1 *A person should consider us in this way.* His topic is how Christians should relate to their ministers. *servants of Christ.* Under Christ's authority, doing the work given him or her by Christ. *managers.* Literally, stewards. In a Greek household this was the slave who administered all the affairs of the family. *God's mysteries.* As in 2:7, these are the plans of God once known only to himself, but now revealed to all. It is the minister's task to make known these mysteries.

4:2 *faithful.* The key requirement for a steward is that he be reliable in looking after his master's affairs. But the question is: Who will decide if the steward has been faithful? Paul answers this in verse 4.

4:3 *evaluated by you.* As becomes evident, especially in 2 Corinthians, the Corinthians were very critical of Paul. *I don't even evaluate myself.* In fact, neither the Corinthians nor Paul himself is fit to judge his faithfulness as a steward of God. God is the only judge of that, and Paul is content to rest in that knowledge and not let the criticism bother him.

4:4 *not justified by this.* Paul has no secret guilt, but this is not a sign of innocence as much as of ignorance. Justification comes not because of innocence (no one is without sin), but by grace as a result of Christ's atoning death.

4:5 *before the Lord comes.* At the second coming of Christ, the Day of Judgment will occur. Paul cautions against making premature judg-ments. Let the Lord judge. He is the only one able to do it properly, since he alone can see not only a person's actions but also a person's motives. *intentions.* Not just actions but one's personal intentions will be made plain when Christ returns.

4:6 *inflated with pride in favor of one person over another.* Paul and Apollos are col-leagues—servants of the same Christ. It is silly to set one against the other. To do this clearly is a matter of pride.

4:8 *Already.* The Corinthians are acting as if the new age had already arrived—that they had come into the fullness of God, into their inher-itance as children of God and into the kingdom of God itself. *we also could reign with you.* Paul wishes they were right because, in fact, his present experience was quite grim (vv. 11–12; 2 Cor. 6:4–10).

4:9 *condemned to die.* The image is of the tri-umphal return of a Roman general who parades his trophies before the people. At the end of the procession marches a band of cap-tives, who will be taken into the arena to fight and die.

4:10 *fools for Christ.* By the standards of the world's wisdom, Paul is indeed foolish. *you are wise in Christ.* In ironic contrast Paul points out that the Corinthians, in their worldly wis-dom, are acting as if they are wise and superior. *We are weak.* In God's economy, weakness is strength. In the suffering Savior one finds the model for the Christian life.

4:12 we labor. As Paul did in Corinth, making tents with Priscilla and Aquila (Acts 18:3; 20:34).

4:13 the world's garbage. The word translated "garbage" refers to the dirt and filth removed in cleaning; such a task was given to the most worthless people.

4:14 to shame you. Indeed, the Corinthians ought to be blushing in acute distress over how far they have departed from Christ's intentions. Still, it is not shame Paul intends. **warn.** The word means, "to admonish" as a father might do, in hopes that his children will see the error of their ways and change.

4:15 instructors. Tutors, Christian leaders who instruct them in the faith (3:6,8,10). **I have fathered you.** Paul led them to faith in Christ.

4:16 be imitators of me. If they need a model of how to live the Christian life, they can look to Paul: a servant eager to do Christ's bidding and a man who walks in the footsteps of a despised, crucified Savior (vv. 11–12).

4:17 This is why. Because Paul wishes them to imitate him and because he himself cannot come yet (though he is planning a trip), he will send Timothy who will model for them the Christian life. **my beloved and faithful child.** Paul discipled Timothy and treated him as if he were his own son.

4:20 kingdom of God. The reign of God which is already here but not yet in fullness. **not in talk but in power.** It is one thing to make loud boasts and claim great wisdom. It is quite another to live out the power of God. They will see that power expressed in Paul's judgment if they do not repent.

Sexual Immorality

Scripture 1 Corinthians 6:12–20

LAST WEEK *In last week's session, we considered how pride and "power plays" were causing conflict in the Corinthian church. We were reminded that God is the source and giver of all our gifts and talents; therefore we should always rely on him and not on ourselves. This week we will look at some problems with sexual immorality in the Corinthian church—problems that may throw some light on our own generation's sexual permissiveness.*

 ## Ice-Breaker Connect With Your Group (15 minutes)

Leader
Open with a word of prayer, and then introduce any new people. To help new group members get acquainted, remember to do all three Ice-Breaker questions.

Some of the self-control issues we deal with are less serious, dealing with things that are permissible but not helpful. Other issues are more serious, dealing with sins (like sexual immorality) that are harmful both physically and spiritually. In this passage Paul addresses both areas of self-control: not allowing ourselves to be controlled either by non-helpful habits or by serious sin. Take turns sharing your responses to the following questions about the important topic of self-control.

1. What "permissible" but "not helpful" thing can you think of in your life that sometimes threatens to control you?

2. Do you enjoy trying out the latest diet plans and exercise programs? What do you think it takes to make these really work?

3. How seriously do you take what you do with your body?

Bible Study Read Scripture and Discuss (30 minutes)

Leader
Select a member of the group ahead of time to read aloud the Scripture passage. Then discuss the Questions for Interaction, dividing into subgroups of three to six.

Sexual addictions are rampant in our society. We have "adult "book-stores" in most towns and pornography is the most profitable business on the Internet. This same kind of addiction was evident in Corinth as well. Read 1 Corinthians 6:12–20 and note how the same truth that Paul gave the Corinthians must still guide us today.

Sexual Immorality

[12]"Everything is permissible for me," but not everything is helpful. "Everything is permissible for me," but I will not be brought under the control of anything. [13]"Foods for the stomach and the stomach for foods," but God will do away with both of them. The body is not for sexual immorality but for the Lord, and the Lord for the body. [14]God raised up the Lord and will also raise us up by His power. [15]Do you not know that your bodies are the members of Christ? So should I take the members of Christ and make them members of a prostitute? Absolutely not! [16]Do you not know that anyone joined to a prostitute is one body with her? For it says, The two will become one flesh. [17]But anyone joined to the Lord is one spirit with Him.

[18]Flee from sexual immorality! "Every sin a person can commit is outside the body," but the person who is sexually immoral sins against his own body. [19]Do you not know that your body is a sanctuary of the Holy Spirit who is in you, whom you have from God? You are not your own, [20]for you were bought at a price; therefore glorify God in your body.

1 Corinthians 6:12–20

Questions for Interaction

Leader
Refer to the Summary and Study Notes at the end of this session as needed. If 30 minutes is not enough time to answer all of the questions in this section, conclude the Bible Study by answering questions 6 and 7.

1. In which of the following ways are you most likely to abuse your body?

   ○ Getting too little sleep.
   ○ Eating too much of the unhealthy stuff.
   ○ Living a fast-paced, tense lifestyle.
   ○ Overdosing on caffeine.
   ○ Smoking.
   ○ Drinking too much.
   ○ Other _____.

2. What attitude about sex do some in the Corinthian church seem to be manifesting, as evidenced by these sayings that Paul responds to (see notes on vv. 12–13)?

3. From this passage, what are Paul's arguments against sexual immorality? Which one is most convincing to you?

4. What connection is there between the "spiritual" and the "physical"? How does this make sexual sin unique?

5. What does it mean, "your body is a sanctuary of the Holy Spirit" (v. 19)? What implication does this have when you abuse your body in any way?

6. How well have you been caring for the sanctuary of the Holy Spirit that is your body? What lifestyle changes do you need to make to take better care of your body?

7. What price is Paul referring to when he writes, "You are not your own, for you were bought at a price" (vv. 19–20)? How do you feel about being "owned" in this way?

Going Deeper   If your group has time and/or wants a challenge, go on to this question.

8. What should Christians be doing to convey to our modern culture the view of sexuality that Paul taught?

 Caring Time Apply the Lesson and Pray for One Another (15 minutes)

Comfort and encourage one another with this time of sharing and prayer. Begin by sharing your responses to the following questions. Be sure to offer any other prayer requests and concerns before closing in prayer.

Leader
Encourage everyone to participate in this important time and be sure that each group member is receiving prayer support. Continue to pray for the empty chair in the closing group prayer.

1. How would you describe your spiritual health?

   ○ I just had a physical and all is well.
   ○ I am getting over the flu.
   ○ I think I am all right, but I hate to go to the doctor to find out.
   ○ I work out every day, and I hope to be in shape soon.
   ○ Other _____.

2. How can this group support you in prayer regarding the needed lifestyle changes you mentioned in answering question 6?

3. Where could God specifically use you and/or the group to bring a healthier view of sexuality to the culture? If you have children, how do you need to better educate them about God's plan for sex? Pray that God would give you the boldness and wisdom to do so.

NEXT WEEK *Today we looked at some warnings that Paul gave the Corinthian church on sexual immorality. We were reminded that our body is "a sanctuary of the Holy Spirit," so we need to have a lifestyle that glorifies God. In the coming week, make at least one change toward a healthier and purer lifestyle. Next week we will follow this up by considering Paul's views on marriage.*

Notes on 1 Corinthians 6:12–20

Summary: Paul now tackles head-on the confusion that exists in the newly formed Corinthian church over the question of sexuality. In looking at this section, it is important to remember what was said in the introduction to this study on the moral atmosphere of Corinth. The Greek author Pausanias describes 26 pagan shrines and temples that were in Corinth, including the great temples of Apollo and Aphrodite. Temple prostitution was a central part of the worship of these deities. The city developed a worldwide reputation for vice and debauchery. We might think that turning from this might be automatic when people in Corinth became Christians. But there was simply no connection in their history between spirituality and sexual restraint. They had to be taught this, and that is what Paul sought to do in these passages. This is actually Part 2 of that discussion. In 5:1–13 he addressed a specific problem (incest). Here he discusses another problem (prostitution) and by so doing lays down some general guidelines. In chapter 7 he will discuss the positive side of sexuality when he examines marriage.

6:12 *"Everything is permissible for me."* This was possibly the slogan of a libertarian party at Corinth, which felt that, since the body was insignificant (in comparison with the "spirit"), it did not really matter what one did. In one sense, this slogan is true. It defines the nature of Christian freedom, and Paul does not disagree with it. He does, however, take issue with how the slogan has come to be used; that is, as an excuse for indulgent and promiscuous behavior. He argues that while everything may be permissible, not everything is good (much less beneficial). **not everything is helpful / I will not be brought under the control.** The principle of freedom must be shaped by the principle of love. We should ask: (1) Is what I am doing good for others or myself; and (2) What does my activity show about whom or what I honor as Lord? Otherwise, Christian

freedom becomes a cover for self-indulgence. God's law is still important as a means of illustrating what love looks like (Rom. 13:9–10). To indulge one's appetites in unsuitable ways is to put oneself under the power of that appetite, and to open the possibility of slavery to a harmful habit. So such license is not really Christian liberty because it produces bondage.

6:13 *"Foods for the stomach and the stomach for foods."* Here also in this second slogan, the low view of the Gnostics toward the body asserts itself. Paul does not directly dispute this slogan, either. Food laws do not bind Christians. Diet is a matter of indifference—especially in that it has no impact on one's salvation. **body.** The stomach is one thing (it will pass away in the natural course of things), but the body is something else (it will live on). "Body" means for Paul not just bones and tissues, but the whole person. What the Corinthians failed to see was that the body is the means by which one serves the Lord. Therefore, it is to be used to honor God. *not for sexual immorality.* Paul now qualifies his acceptance of the slogan. It appears the Corinthians were arguing that in the same way it was permissible for Christians to satisfy their physical appetite without regard to the Law, so they had the right to satisfy their sexual appetite with the same disregard of the Law. This Paul emphatically denies.

6:14 *will also raise us up.* In fact, the body will be resurrected, as was the Lord's body. (His was not a "spiritual" resurrection. Jesus' body was missing from the tomb.) Since our bodies will be resurrected for eternity, they surely should not be used for sexual immorality.

6:15 Prostitutes were often associated with pagan religious ceremonies. Paul's argument, based on the Christian's spiritual union with Christ, implies that this is the nature of the prostitution in view here (the same problem surfaces in 8:1–13 regarding the eating of food used in these temples). Paul quotes Genesis 2:24 to indicate that the sex act implies a spiritual union between the participants. Hence, to have sex with these prostitutes implied a union with their god as well, violating the spiritual bonding the Christian has made with Christ (v. 18). *prostitute.* In addition to this, the Christian marriage was to reflect the relationship of Christ and the church. (Eph. 5:25-29). So while Paul may particularly have had the temple prostitutes in mind, he probably was referring to prostitutes in general as well, which would have been numerous in a port city like Corinth. The Corinthians may have been arguing for the "right" to engage in sexually oriented religious activities. Since the body of the Christian belongs to the Lord and is for his use, it is incon-

ceivable ("Absolutely not!") that it be handed over to a prostitute.

6:16 *Do you not know.* This is no new principle which Paul proposes, as he shows by quoting Genesis 2:24. *joined.* In its literal use, this word referred to gluing things together. In its metaphorical sense here, it points to the strong bonding between two people that takes place as a result of intercourse. Intercourse is not merely an inconsequential physical act. In fact, it is akin to the bonding between the believer and the Lord, as Paul shows in verse 17 (where he uses this same word). *one body with her.* Such uniting with a prostitute makes the two one flesh. This stands in contrast to the kind of uniting appropriate for holy people, including uniting with the Lord (v. 17).

6:18 *Flee.* The temptation to sexual sin was so overwhelming in Corinth that Paul uses this strong verb by way of command. The sexual impulse is so powerful that it is generally useless to fight it. One must flee from those situations that arouse it wrongly. *sexual immorality.* Not unexpectedly (given the nature of life in Corinth), the Corinthians were confused about their sexuality. In chapter 7, it appears that many wondered if marriage should be avoided, and whether sexual intercourse was to be shunned between marriage partners. So here, the position that Paul is arguing against might be that since it was the duty of a husband to keep his wife "pure," he could occasionally find sexual satisfaction with a harlot if necessary. *sins against his own body.* Such a person betrays his body by using it in a way for which it was not designed. The result of such abuse is frequently contact with sexually transmitted diseases, which can bring on long term or permanent health problems. Other abuses and addictions, such as use of drugs, alcohol and tobacco, or under and overeating also have long term effects on our bodies, but the spiritual problems brought on by sexual sins seem to be of a unique nature, perhaps because of the fact that the church is to be the bride of Christ, and thus Christians are to model that faithful and pure bride.

6:19 In 3:16, Paul pointed out that the church was the dwelling place of the Holy Spirit. Here he points to the parallel truth: the Holy Spirit also dwells in the individual believer.

6:20 *bought at a price.* The image is of ransoming slaves from their bondage. In the same way, Christ has paid the ransom price in order to free Christians from the bondage of sin. Out of sheer gratitude, Christians ought to flee sin. Out of sheer common sense, they ought to flee sin, lest they fall back into bondage.

Marriage

Scripture 1 Corinthians 7:1–16,32–35

> **LAST WEEK** *Our discussion last week focused on the lifestyle that we are to follow as Christians. We were reminded by Paul to "flee from sexual immorality" (6:18) and glorify God with our bodies. These words of Paul are still relevant, as today's society is facing the same moral decline. This week we will go a step further and see what Paul's writings on marriage have to say about the status of that sacred institution.*

Ice-Breaker Connect With Your Group (15 minutes)

Our upbringing, the media and society are a few of the things that influence our view of marriage and the commitment it requires. There are many who would like to change the definition of marriage and downplay its importance. Paul would have us turn our hearts back to God, the Creator of marriage, to rediscover this sacred institution's true definition and purpose. Take turns now sharing your thoughts about marriage.

Leader
Choose one or two of the Ice-Breaker questions. If you have a new group member, you may want to do all three. Remember to stick closely to the three-part agenda and the time allowed for each segment.

1. When you were a teenager, who had the marriage that you secretly hoped your own marriage would one day be like?

   ○ My parents.
   ○ An older sibling and spouse.
   ○ A neighbor couple.
   ○ A celebrity couple.
   ○ A couple at church.
   ○ Nobody.
   ○ Other _____.

2. Finish this sentence: "The most important thing about marriage to me is ... "

3. If married, tell your "love story"—how you met, how you knew this person was "the one" and when and where you got married. If single, share what you know about your parents' love story.

Bible Study Read Scripture and Discuss (30 minutes)

In the following passage, Paul teaches us about sharing our life with a mate. Marriage was the first "community" God established on this earth. This shows the importance that God places on the institution of marriage. Read 1 Corinthians 7:1–16,32–35 and note what is involved in being fully committed to a marriage relationship.

Leader

Select three members of the group ahead of time to read aloud the Scripture passage. Have one member read verses 1–7; the second read verses 8–16; and the third read verses 32–35. Then discuss the Questions for Interaction, dividing into subgroups of three to six.

Marriage

Reader One: 7 About the things you wrote: "It is good for a man not to have relations with a woman." ²But because of sexual immorality, each man should have his own wife, and each woman should have her own husband. ³A husband should fulfill his marital duty to his wife, and likewise a wife to her husband. ⁴A wife does not have authority over her own body, but her husband does. Equally, a husband does not have authority over his own body, but his wife does. ⁵Do not deprive one another—except when you agree, for a time, to devote yourselves to prayer. Then come together again; otherwise, Satan may tempt you because of your lack of self-control. ⁶I say this as a concession, not as a command. ⁷I wish that all people were just like me. But each has his own gift from God, one this and another that.

Reader Two: ⁸I say to the unmarried and to widows: It is good for them if they remain as I am. ⁹But if they do not have self-control, they should marry, for it is better to marry than to burn with desire. ¹⁰I command the married—not I, but the Lord—a wife is not to leave her husband. ¹¹But if she does leave, she must remain unmarried or be reconciled to her husband—and a husband is not to leave his wife. ¹²But to the rest I, not the Lord, say: If any brother has an unbelieving wife, and she is willing to live with him, he must not leave her. ¹³Also, if any woman has an unbelieving husband, and he is willing to live with her, she must not leave her husband. ¹⁴For the unbelieving husband is sanctified by the wife, and the unbelieving wife is sanctified by the Christian husband. Otherwise your children would be unclean, but now they are holy. ¹⁵But if the unbeliever leaves, let him leave. A brother or a sister is not bound in such cases. God has called you to peace. ¹⁶For you, wife, how do you know whether you will save your husband? Or you, husband, how do you know whether you will save your wife?

Reader Three: ³²I want you to be without concerns. An unmarried man is concerned about the things of the Lord—how he may please the Lord. ³³But a married man is concerned about the things of the world—how he may please his wife— ³⁴and he is divided. An unmarried woman or a virgin is concerned about the things of the Lord, so that she may be holy both in body and in spirit. But a married woman is concerned about the things of the world—how she may please her husband. [35]Now I am saying this for your own benefit, not to put a restraint on you, but because of what is proper, and so that you may be devoted to the Lord without distraction.

1 Corinthians 7:1–16,32–35

Questions for Interaction

Leader
Refer to the Summary and Study Notes at the end of this session as needed. If 30 minutes is not enough time to answer all of the questions in this section, conclude the Bible Study by answering questions 6 and 7.

1. From what you read here, what word would you use to describe Paul's attitude about sex and marriage?

   O Prudish.
   O Pragmatic.
   O Dispassionate.
   O Understanding.
   O Chauvinistic.
   O Spiritual.
   O Other _____.

2. Which of the issues Paul discusses here touches your own life most personally?

   O Sexual duties and privileges in marriage.
   O Sexual self-control.
   O The advantages of the single life.
   O Divorce.
   O Living with a nonbeliever.
   O Other _____.

3. What danger does Paul say there is with sexually depriving your mate? What advantage can you see to abstaining from sex by mutual consent as a spiritual discipline (v. 5)?

4. What obligation does a believing spouse have to a nonbelieving mate (vv. 12–14)? What does it mean for a nonbeliever to be "sanctified" by a believing spouse (see notes on v. 14)?

5. What does Paul say are the advantages of a Christian remaining single (vv. 32–35)? What advantages does he see in marrying? Are there advantages and disadvantages of both lifestyles that he does not mention here?

6. Whether single or married, who should have first place in your life (v. 35)? How is your own marital status affecting your service for the Lord?

7. What percentage of your focus in life is on "the things of the Lord," and what percentage is on "the things of the world"? What is one thing you could do to change the balance to a healthier percentage?

8. What is Paul saying to couples whose sexual appetites differ? Do his words mean that a person should always respond to his or her spouse's desire? If you and your spouse are both "part owners" of your body, how should "corporate decisions" be made about sexual activity?

Caring Time Apply the Lesson and Pray for One Another (15 minutes)

Knowing that God is merciful and forgiving, come before him now in this time of sharing and prayer. Encourage and support one another so you can each focus your life on "the things of the Lord."

1. What season are you experiencing in your spiritual life right now?

   ○ The warmth of summer.
   ○ The dead of winter.
   ○ The new life of spring.
   ○ The changes of fall.

Leader
Be sure to save at least 15 minutes for this time of prayer and encouragement. Continue to encourage group members to invite new people to the group. Remind them that this group is for learning and sharing, but also for reaching out to others.

2. How can this group be supportive of those group members or others who are going through a divorce?

3. How can this group pray for you as a single or married person in relation to your service for the Lord (remember your answers to both questions 6 and 7)?

NEXT WEEK *Today we looked at Paul's views on marriage, as he tried to clear up some misunderstandings in the Corinthian church regarding sexuality. We were reminded that we need to take seriously the commitments of marriage and that marriage is a calling and a gift from God. Next week we will focus on Paul's example of discipline in the Christian life and how important this can be in spreading the Gospel.*

Summary: Having just dealt with the issue of proper sexual morality from the perspective of when to avoid improper sexual contact , Paul now goes on to speak of when it is appropriate—in the marriage bed. Sex in the context of marriage is appropriate and good, and can help a person from straying into sexually promiscuous behavior with someone else. All that he says here is predicated on two assumptions: (1) one's first loyalty is always to God as he was revealed in Jesus Christ, and (2) Christ would soon return. We should always be serving Christ with the expectation that he could return any day, any hour. Not even something as good as marriage should be allowed to get in the way of that.

7:1 *you wrote.* Up to this point Paul has been dealing with matters reported to him, but now he responds to a series of concerns about which the Corinthian Christians have written. ***to have relations with a woman.*** The phrase is literally, "to touch a woman," and is a common euphemism for sexual intercourse.

7:2 *have his own wife/her own husband.* The phrase means "to be married," or "to have sexual relations."

7:5 Abstinence is allowed under two conditions: both partners agree, and it is for a limited time. ***deprive.*** Literally, "rob." For one partner to opt out of sexual relations under the guise of spirituality is a form of robbery. ***prayer.*** The purpose of such abstinence is prayer. ***lack of self-control.*** Paul assumes that a couple would not be married in the first place if they did not feel any sexual desire, and thus they ought to fulfill such desires legitimately, lest they be tempted to adultery.

7:7 *were just like me.* That is, celibate; though Paul is not advocating celibacy, as much as resistance against inappropriate sexual expression. ***gift.*** Paul states that celibacy is a spiritual gift.

7:8 *remain as I am.* While Paul may always have been a bachelor, it is more likely that he was a widower, since it was quite rare for a rabbi to be unmarried. In fact, marriage was virtually obligatory for a Jewish man.

7:9 *do not have self-control.* Abstinence would be a particular problem for those who had once experienced an active married life. ***to burn.*** When one is consumed with desire, that preoccupation makes it difficult to lead a devoted Christian life.

7:10 *not I, but the Lord.* Paul is probably referring to statements by Jesus, as in Mark 10:2–12. ***not to leave her husband.*** Despite his preference for the single life, Paul forbids those who are already married to be divorced.

7:11 *if she does leave.* Paul recognizes that sometimes divorce does happen among Christian couples.

7:12 *I, not the Lord.* Paul means that Jesus did not say anything about mixed marriages—and so Paul cannot refer back to a saying of his (as he did in v. 10).

7:14 *sanctified.* Not in the sense of having effected their salvation. Paul is arguing against the view that within mixed marriages the Christian partner is defiled. The contrary is true. ***they are holy.*** In the Jewish community, children of Jewish parents are considered a part of the covenant, and Paul probably means this here.

7:15 Should the non-Christian partner leave, the prohibition against divorce does not apply.

7:34 *and he is divided.* The married man is rightly concerned about how to please the Lord, and equally right in his concern to please his wife. This is the problem: how to be fully faithful to both legitimate commitments. *a married woman.* The same is true of a married woman: her attention is divided in a way not true of a single woman.

7:35 *not to put a restraint on you.* Literally, "not to put a halter around your neck," as one would do in order to domesticate an animal.

Disciplines for the Race

Scripture 1 Corinthians 9:19–27

LAST WEEK *We looked at the subject of marriage in last week's session, and gained some understanding of Paul's views on marriage and the importance of that sacred institution. We were reminded that, whatever our marital status is, we should wholeheartedly serve the Lord. This week we will examine what Paul says about discipline in the Christian life and being a powerful witness.*

Ice-Breaker Connect With Your Group (15 minutes)

Playing a piano concerto, running a marathon, performing the lead role in a play—these are all accomplishments that require much self-discipline. We admire people who can do these things, but how often do we think about the discipline needed to live the Christian life successfully? Sharing your thoughts and experiences about self-discipline.

Leader
Open with a word of prayer, and then introduce and welcome any new group members. Choose one, two or all three Ice-Breaker questions to get started.

1. When you were in high school, in which of the following extracurricular activities were you most active?

   ○ Sports.
   ○ Band or choir.
   ○ Drama.
   ○ Chess or debate.
   ○ Cheerleading or drill team.
   ○ Smoking in the rest rooms.
   ○ Other _____.

2. What disciplines were necessary in order for you to participate in the activity you listed in question 1 above? How good were you at those disciplines?

3. What requires the most discipline for you?

○ Eating properly.
○ Getting enough exercise.
○ Taking time for my family.
○ Getting projects done around the house.
○ Other _____.

Bible Study Read Scripture and Discuss (30 minutes)

Self-control is a popular theme in Paul's letters. He emphasizes it as a defining characteristic for the follower of Christ. However, as we have all experienced, at times it is hard to maintain. Read 1 Corinthians 9:19–27 and note how we can encourage each other to live a disciplined life and have self-control.

Leader
Select two members of the group ahead of time to read aloud the Scripture passage. Then discuss the Questions for Interaction, dividing into subgroups of three to six.

Disciplines for the Race

Reader One: [19]For although I am free from all people, I have made myself a slave to all, in order to win more people.

Reader Two: [20]To the Jews I became like a Jew, to win Jews; to those under the law, like one under the law—though I myself am not under the law—to win those under the law.

Reader One: [21]To those who are outside the law, like one outside the law—not being outside God's law, but under the law of Christ—to win those outside the law.

Reader Two: [22]To the weak I became weak, in order to win the weak. I have become all things to all people, so that I may by all means save some. [23]Now I do all this because of the gospel, that I may become a partner in its benefits.

Reader One: [24]Do you not know that the runners in a stadium all race, but only one receives the prize? Run in such a way that you may win. [25]Now everyone who competes exercises self-control in everything. However, they do it to receive a perishable crown, but we an imperishable one. [26]Therefore I do not run like one who runs aimlessly, or box like one who beats the air. [27]Instead, I discipline my body and bring it under strict control, so that after preaching to others, I myself will not be disqualified.

1 Corinthians 9:19–27

Questions for Interaction

Leader
Refer to the Summary and Study Notes at the end of this session as needed. If 30 minutes is not enough time to answer all of the questions in this section, conclude the Bible Study by answering questions 6 and 7.

1. What are you most likely to become a "slave" to?

   ○ Fashion.
   ○ The wishes of the opposite sex.
   ○ Taking care of others.
   ○ My addictions.
   ○ Watching television.
   ○ Wanting to be liked.
   ○ Work.
   ○ Other _____.

2. What does it mean that Paul made himself "a slave to all" (v. 19) in order to win people to Christ? How is that different than being a spineless chameleon who tries to be liked by everyone?

3. How is the Christian life like a race, according to Paul? What is a difference that Paul points out? Do you see any other differences?

4. What are some disciplines one must maintain in order to run in a race? What are some disciplines one must maintain in order to live a vital Christian life?

5. What does it mean to "win" in the Christian life? How is that different than the world's definition of winning? What is the nature of the "crown" we seek?

6. If you compared your spiritual life right now to a track race (as Paul was doing in vv. 24–27), where would you be right now?

   ○ Sitting on the sidelines.
   ○ Warming up.
   ○ At the starting block.
   ○ Giving it your all.
   ○ Back in the pack and "sucking wind."
   ○ Gutting it out.
   ○ Giving up.
   ○ Pushing for the finish line, which is near.

7. What disciplines are you practicing in your "race" right now? What disciplines do you most need to work on?

8. When is it good or helpful to act like those around you in order to win them for Christ? What might be some examples where that would be diluting the Gospel?

 Caring Time Apply the Lesson and Pray for One
Another (15 minutes)

Take some time now to encourage one another to keep running to the finish line and the "imperishable" crown that is the prize for our faith-fulness and discipline. Begin by giving your answers to the following questions. Then share prayer requests and close with prayer.

Leader
Continue to encourage group members to invite new people to the group. Close the group prayer by thanking God for each member and for this time together.

1. This past week, did you feel more like you were winning the race of life or getting so far behind that you will never catch up, and why?

2. Who are those around you (v. 22) who need Christ and for whom this group might pray?

3. How can this group pray for you in developing the spiritual disciplines you need in order to "win" the race?

NEXT WEEK *Today we considered the importance of discipline in the Christian life. Through Paul's example, we saw how important this characteristic can be in spreading the Gospel. In the coming week, follow through on your answer to question 7 and pick at least one spiritual discipline to add to your daily routine. Next week we will discover what Paul said about the nature of the Lord's Supper and what it means to the Christian community.*

Summary: Paul has been talking about what it means to be free, and how as an apostle he has voluntarily given up some of his freedoms in order to advance the Gospel. Here he writes more specifically about what this has meant for him. Paul is free, but he restricts his personal behavior for the sake of others. Thus, he would not eat idol-meat when he was with Jews, legalists or the weak. The implication is that he could (and probably did) eat idol-meat with Gentiles (though not at pagan temples). Next he switches to the image of a race in the Greek games. Athletes must voluntarily restrict their freedom to spend time in training. They must discipline themselves to give up certain things they like and to work when they would rather rest. They do this to win the crown awarded for winning the race. Christians must show similar discipline, but they do so to win an eternal crown, rather than a temporal one. That should motivate the follower of Christ even more to pursue these disciplines.

9:19 *although I am free.* In verse 1, this appears to have referred to Paul's freedom from dietary concerns based on religious scruples. While it carries the same meaning here, it also includes the fact that since he refuses financial support from those he teaches, he is obligated to no system or group. *I have made myself a slave.* Since Paul is free, he can voluntarily enslave himself to others in order that he may win them to Christ.

9:20 *I became like a Jew.* Paul was a Jew by birth, but as a result of his conversion he was freed from the Law and its obligations. Yet in order to win other Jews, in certain instances he behaved as if he were back under the Law—though understanding all the time that this was not the means by which he came to know God. An example of this was when he participated with four men in a Jewish vow and rite of purification, in order to try (unsuccessfully) to appease some Jewish opponents in Jerusalem (Acts 21:21–26).

9:21 Likewise, in other instances, he behaves as if he were outside the Law. Yet so as not to leave the Corinthians with the impression that a Christian could do whatever he or she wanted without regard to its morality, he also points to Christ's law (the law of love) to which he is obe-dient. *but under the law of Christ.* Paul's freedom is not license. Christ's law, the law of love (John 15:12; James 2:8), governs all he does. This implies a moral responsibility to be actively engaged in continually serving the concerns and interests of others rather than living simply for one's own self-interests.

9:22 *the weak.* Those with weak consciences (8:7–13) who are not yet free from legalism or from the power of paganism. Paul voluntarily abstained from that which offended the weak. *save some.* The real issue is salvation, not just persuading people to join the church.

9:24 *only one receives the prize.* When only one receives the prize, a person has to work that much harder to win, knowing that others are also working hard. While it is not true that there can be only one "winner" in the Christian life, one should nevertheless work as hard and discipline oneself as much as if that were true.

9:25 The emphasis is on the self-control that is needed to win in the games. *crown.* The Christian's crown is eternal life.

9:26 A runner in a race cannot simply run in any direction he or she chooses. The runner must stay on the course. No boxer swings wildly at the air, but concentrates on his opponent. *runs aimlessly.* Such a runner has no fixed goal. Paul's activities (which he has outlined in this chapter) are not without a point. Everything he does is for the sake of the Gospel. *beats the air.* In the same way that he pictured pointless running, now he switches to the image of fruitless boxing.

9:27 Paul applies the boxing imagery to himself as he wraps up the discussion of "freedom." Just as it is important for him to discipline his bodily urges (for food—8:1–13; for sex—6:12–20), so that he might be faithful to Christ's call, so too the Corinthians must exercise their Christian freedom in light of their responsibility to love. Otherwise, both he and they might be disqualified from God's race, like runners who left the track. Love, not "knowledge" (8:1), is the essential demonstration of true faith. *discipline my body.* The comparison is to a master disciplining a slave. As Christians our bodies have to be made to be our slaves instead of vice versa. When we follow every impulse, every physical desire of our bodies, we become slaves to our bodies, and our cravings can destroy us. Instead we need to make our bodies serve our overall spiritual well-being.

The Lord's Supper

Scripture 1 Corinthians 11:17–34

LAST WEEK *In last week's session, we considered the important role of discipline in living the Christian life and how our example can be a powerful witness. Paul reminded us that we should be more motivated "to run the race" than those with earthly goals, because our reward will be the "imperishable crown" of eternal life. This week we will consider the Lord's Supper and what it means for Christian community.*

Ice-Breaker Connect With Your Group (15 minutes)

Leader
Open with a word of prayer, and be sure to welcome and introduce new group members. Choose one, two or all three of the Ice-Breaker questions.

Most of us would agree with the saying that "No man [or woman] is an island." We need each other and enjoy being part of a group, like this one. On the other hand, when we feel rejected it can be very difficult. Take turns sharing your unique experiences with group dynamics.

1. When you were in high school, which of the following divisions or cliques had a prominent role in your school? Which ones did you feel you were part of?

    ○ The jocks.
    ○ The popular kids.
    ○ The nerds.
    ○ The hoods or rebels.
    ○ The teachers' pets.
    ○ Other _____.

2. When you don't feel like you are part of a group, what are you most likely to do?

   ○ Sulk and feel rejected.
   ○ Do everything to please people so I can get in.
   ○ Start my own group.
   ○ Not worry about it—I do my own thing.
   ○ Figure it's their loss.
   ○ Other _____.

3. At your family meals, does everyone eat on his or her own schedule or do you all eat together?
   When was the last time you really enjoyed each other's fellowship around a meal? (If you live alone,
   answer this one according to the family in which you were raised.)

 Bible Study Read Scripture and Discuss (30 minutes)

In our passage today, Paul gives specific instructions on how the Lord's
Supper is to be celebrated. He reminded the Corinthians that it is to be
a sacred time of remembering what Jesus did for us in his sacrificial
suffering and death. It should be a time of unity, and not division. Read
1 Corinthians 11:17–34 and note how we should honor the celebration
of the Lord's Supper and remember how Jesus died for each one of us.

Leader
Select two members
of the group ahead of
time to read aloud the
Scripture passage.
Have one person read
verses 17–24, and the
other read verses
25–34. Then discuss
the Questions for
Interaction, dividing
into subgroups of
three to six.

The Lord's Supper

Reader One: [17]Now in giving the following instruction I do not praise
you, since you come together not for the better but for
the worse. [18]For, to begin with, I hear that when you come together as a church there
are divisions among you, and in part I believe it. [19]There must, indeed, be factions
among you, so that the approved among you may be recognized. [20]Therefore when you
come together in one place, it is not really to eat the Lord's Supper. [21]For in eating,
each one takes his own supper ahead of others, and one person is hungry while
another is drunk! [22]Don't you have houses to eat and drink in? Or do you look down on
the church of God and embarrass those who have nothing? What should I say to you?
Should I praise you? I do not praise you for this! [23]For I received from the Lord what I
also passed on to you: on the night when He was betrayed, the Lord Jesus took bread,
[24]gave thanks, broke it, and said, "This is My body, which is for you. Do this in remembrance of Me."

Reader Two: [25]In the same way He also took the cup, after supper, and said, "This cup is the new
covenant in My blood. Do this, as often as you drink it, in remembrance of Me." [26]For
as often as you eat this bread and drink the cup, you proclaim the Lord's death until
He comes. [27]Therefore, whoever eats the bread or drinks the cup of the Lord in an
unworthy way will be guilty of sin against the body and blood of the Lord. [28]So a man

should examine himself; in this way he should eat of the bread and drink of the cup. [29]For whoever eats and drinks without recognizing the body, eats and drinks judgment on himself. [30]This is why many are sick and ill among you, and many have fallen asleep. [31]If we were properly evaluating ourselves, we would not be judged, [32]but when we are judged, we are disciplined by the Lord, so that we may not be condemned with the world. [33]Therefore, my brothers, when you come together to eat, wait for one another. [34]If anyone is hungry, he should eat at home, so that you can come together and not cause judgment. And I will give instructions about the other matters whenever I come.

1 Corinthians 11:17–34

Questions for Interaction

Leader
Refer to the Summary and Study Notes at the end of this session as needed. If 30 minutes is not enough time to answer all of the questions in this section, conclude the Bible Study by answering questions 6 and 7.

1. Are there divisions in your own church? What is the basis of each (age difference, following certain personalities, socioeconomic status, etc.)? Which is your group and from which do feel excluded?

2. How were the divisions in the Corinthian church affecting the way they celebrated the Lord's Supper? What problems were being created? Why was this especially inappropriate (see notes on vv. 21–22)?

3. What are Christians proclaiming when they celebrate the Lord's Supper together? What helps you to be more mindful of this, so that the Lord's Supper does not become just a meaningless ritual?

4. In this passage, Paul instructs the Corinthians to examine themselves prior to partaking of the Lord's Supper. How is this done? What are the consequences of receiving the Lord's Supper "in an unworthy way" (v. 27)?

5. What does it mean to "recognize the body" (see notes on v. 29)? What does this mean for a church racked by division and dissension?

6. Why is it important for Christians to observe the Lord's Supper? What does Communion mean to you?

7. What do you need to do better in order to celebrate Communion in the most meaningful way?

   ○ Reconcile with some people in my church.
   ○ Develop a greater concern for the people I celebrate with.
   ○ Remember what the Lord's Supper proclaims.
   ○ Be more in touch with Christ's suffering.
   ○ Other _____.

8. What is Paul saying about the physical effects of spiritual actions like abusing Communion? Can such actions really make a person sick? Are there links between spiritual "disease" and physical disease?

Caring Time   Apply the Lesson and Pray for One Another (15 minutes)

Gather around each other now for a time of sharing and prayer, remembering the great sacrifice that Jesus went through for your salvation.

1. How was your walk with the Lord this past week?

2. Remember to pray for the divisions in your own church. What role can this group play in healing those divisions?

3. How can this group pray for you in making the changes you talked about in question 7?

Leader
Have you focused your group on their mission—perhaps by sharing the dream of multiplying into two groups at the end of this study of 1 Corinthians? You may want to celebrate the Lord's Supper as part of the Caring Time this week, depending on your church's policy.

NEXT WEEK *Today we discovered what Paul said about the nature of the Lord's Supper and what it means to the Christian community. We were reminded that we are to honor this celebration and keep it meaningful. In the coming week, spend time reading 1 Corinthians 11:17–34 again, and think about what the Lord's Supper really means to you. Next week we will discuss spiritual gifts and how they can be used to bring people together in service to God.*

Summary: Paul turns to a second, more serious disorder in the Corinthians' worship experience: their abuse of the Lord's Supper. The Lord's Supper was eaten in the context of a community meal—a so-called "love feast" (Jude 12). However, the way they behaved at this meal accented their divisions (rich and poor, followers of one or another leader, etc.) rather than affirmed their unity in Christ. Paul addresses two parts of this problem: the vertical and the horizontal. The theological part of the problem was their failure to honor the Lord. The relational part of the problem was their failure to eat the meal as a loving Christian community. Paul deals with the theological problem in verses 23–26. Then, in verses 27–34, he deals with the relational problem, which he outlines in verses 17–22.

11:17 *not for the better but for the worse.* So flawed are their Communion services that they would be better off not having them. They harm, not heal.

11:18 *I hear.* They had not written Paul about these disorders. Paul had heard what was going on from other sources (1:11; 16:17), and is so shocked that he can't really believe it is as bad as reported ("in part I believe it"). *church.* This word originally referred to a group of citizens who had assembled together for a predetermined purpose. In the Greek Old Testament, this word was used to describe the assembling together of God's people, and it came to have this meaning in the New Testament as well. *divisions.* It seems that class distinction operated at the Lord's Supper—the rich ate abundantly while the poor were hungry. It is also possible that Jewish Christians ate kosher food by themselves apart from Gentile Christians, and that the ascetics sat apart from the libertarians, that those who followed Apollos did not mingle with those who followed Cephas, etc.

11:20 *it is not really to eat the Lord's Supper.* The Corinthians have so badly abused the Communion service that it was more like one of the meals at a pagan temple than a meal held in honor of the Lord.

11:21 *takes his own supper ahead of others.* Apparently, the poor were actually being excluded from the Lord's Supper (v. 33). It is conjectured that the "nobodies" who made up much of the church (1:26) were in fact slaves (7:20–24), and so did not have the freedom to get to church when they wanted to, and the others weren't waiting for them. *hungry/drunk.* The contrast could not be starker. The poor in the church went hungry during this meal, while others indulged themselves to the point of drunkenness.

11:22 If the rich can't wait to indulge in their food and drink, at least they should do this at home and not demean the common meal at church. *embarrass those who have nothing.* The poor feel ashamed that they can't bring the abundant food and drink they see the rich eating. Paul's point is that God accepts the poor, so the rich ought not to make them feel unworthy.

11:23 *on the night when He was betrayed.* The significance of what Jesus did at the Last Supper comes in the context of when it took place—immediately prior to his crucifixion.

11:24 *thanks.* There is nothing unusual in this act. The head of each Jewish household would have done the same thing. *This is My body.* Then Jesus interprets for the disciples the new meaning he is giving to these ordinary acts. He himself will become the Passover lamb for them, to be slain for their sins. *in remembrance.* Paul repeats this phrase twice, so as to stress that the Lord's Supper is a memorial feast (Luke 22:19).

11:25 *in My blood.* The shedding of Jesus' blood inaugurates a new covenant between God and people by which their sins are forgiven as a result of Christ's death in their place.

11:26 This statement is not found in the Gospels. It is Paul's own summary of the meaning of the Lord's Supper. *proclaim the Lord's death.* The Lord's Supper proclaims the fact and meaning of Jesus' death in several ways: the broken bread and outpoured wine symbolically proclaim his death; the words spoken at such a meal (both formally and informally) recall the Crucifixion; and the whole event itself "proclaims" his atoning death. *until He comes.* In this way, Christians recall the story of Jesus' death until he returns.

11:27 *in an unworthy way.* This refers to the disorders in community behavior (vv. 18–22).

They are to scrutinize their lives to see if they are contributing to the divisiveness of the community.

11:28 *should examine himself.* Christians ought to scrutinize their lives to see if they are guilty of divisiveness, of lack of love, of gluttony and drunkenness (i.e., the Corinthian disorders), which might reflect negatively on "the body and the blood of the Lord." Moral perfection is not required, simply moral scrutiny.

11:29 *without recognizing.* When the meal turned into a time of drunkenness, division and gluttony, people lost sight of the meaning of the event. *the body.* Here, "the body" in view is probably the church (as in 12:12), which the Corinthians were abusing. Thus, they would come under the judgment Paul warned about in regard to those who defiled God's temple, the church (3:17).

11:30 Paul contends that the judgment in verse 29 works itself out in concrete, physical ways. *fallen asleep.* A figure of speech for death.

Spiritual Gifts

Scripture 1 Corinthians 12:4–31a

LAST WEEK *Last week we focused on Paul's stern words to the Corinthians about the proper celebration of the Lord's Supper. We were reminded that Communion helps us to remember Jesus' great love for us in that he was willing to suffer and die for our sins. Therefore, we should be careful to observe it with respect and thoughtfulness. This week we will consider the use of spiritual gifts, and how they can be used to build up the church.*

 Ice-Breaker Connect With Your Group (15 minutes)

Leader
Open with a word of prayer. Welcome and introduce new group members. Choose one, two or all three Ice-Breaker questions, depending on your group's needs.

When we think of spiritual gifts we often think of talent and the more obvious things like speaking, singing or writing. But there are so many more spiritual gifts that are just as important. God has given each of us something we can use to help each other along in this life. Take turns sharing some of your thoughts about spiritual gifts.

1. What "hidden" talent do you have that others in this group might not know about?

2. How would you describe yourself as a part of the body?

    ○ An eye—because I am very observant.
    ○ An ear—because I am a good listener.
    ○ A head—because I enjoy exploring things with my mind.
    ○ A hand—because I enjoy lending one to others.
    ○ A mouth—because I am good at expressing myself with words.
    ○ A shoulder—because I have a strong one to lean on or to put to heavy tasks.
    ○ Other _____.

3. What kind of person (expressed in terms of the body parts in question 2) do you most often feel the need for as a friend?

Bible Study Read Scripture and Discuss [30 minutes]

As we are about to read, we all have an important part in this group, in this church and in the overall kingdom of God. If you do not know what that part is, our responsibility as a community group is to help you discover it. As we will see, gifts are best discovered in the context of community. Read 1 Corinthians 12:4–31a and note how each gift builds up the body of Christ.

Leader
Select a member of the group ahead of time to read aloud the Scripture passage. Then discuss the Questions for Interaction, dividing into subgroups of three to six.

Spiritual Gifts

[4]Now there are different gifts, but the same Spirit. [5]There are different ministries, but the same Lord. [6]And there are different activities, but the same God is active in everyone and everything. [7]A manifestation of the Spirit is given to each person to produce what is beneficial:

> [8]to one is given a message of wisdom through the Spirit,
>
> to another, a message of knowledge by the same Spirit,
>
> [9]to another, faith by the same Spirit,
>
> to another, gifts of healing by the one Spirit,
>
> [10]to another, the performing of miracles,
>
> to another, prophecy,
>
> to another, distinguishing between spirits,
>
> to another, different kinds of languages,
>
> to another, interpretation of languages.

[11]But one and the same Spirit is active in all these, distributing to each one as He wills.

[12]For as the body is one and has many parts, and all the parts of that body, though many, are one body—so also is Christ. [13]For we were all baptized by one Spirit into one body—whether Jews or Greeks, whether slaves or free—and we were all made to drink of one Spirit. [14]So the body is not one part but many. [15]If the foot should say, "Because I'm not a hand, I don't belong to the body," in spite of this it still belongs to the body. [16]And if the ear should say, "Because I'm not an eye, I don't belong to the body," in spite of this it still belongs to the body. [17]If the whole body were an eye, where would the hearing be? If the whole were an ear, where would be the sense of smell? [18]But now God has placed the parts, each one of them, in the body just as He wanted. [19]And if they were all the same part, where would the body be? [20]Now there are many parts, yet one body.

[21]So the eye cannot say to the hand, "I don't need you!" nor again the head to the feet, "I don't need you!" [22]On the contrary, all the more, those parts of the body that seem to be weaker are necessary. [23]And those parts of the body that we think to be less honorable, we clothe these with greater honor, and our unpresentable parts have a better presentation. [24]But our presentable parts have no need of clothing. Instead, God has put the body together, giving greater honor to the less honorable, [25]so that there would be no division in the body, but that the members would have the same concern for each other. [26]So if one member suffers, all the members suffer with it; if one member is honored, all the members rejoice with it.

[27]Now you are the body of Christ, and individual members of it. [28]And God has placed these in the church:

> first apostles, second prophets, third teachers, next, miracles,
> then gifts of healing, helping, managing, various kinds of languages.
> [29]Are all apostles?
> Are all prophets?
> Are all teachers? Do all do miracles?
> [30]Do all have gifts of healing?
> Do all speak in languages?
> Do all interpret?

[31]But desire the greater gifts.

1 Corinthians 12:4–31a

Questions for Interaction

Leader
Refer to the Summary and Study Notes at the end of this session as needed. If 30 minutes is not enough time to answer all of the questions in this section, conclude the Bible Study by answering question 7.

1. Comparing your own church fellowship to a body, what kind of body would you say it was?

   ○ A young "buff" hard-body.
   ○ A flexible body—like a gymnast or one of those contortionists.
   ○ A relatively healthy body—but developing a bit of a potbelly.
   ○ A typical middle-aged body—some abilities, but some parts no longer working so well.
   ○ A rather decrepit old body—still functioning, but with a lot of ailments.
   ○ A body in a coma and on life support.

2. Why does Paul use the image of a body to talk about the church? How are the two alike?

3. Who has been given spiritual gifts? Who are they from and for what purpose are they given (v. 7)?

4. What kinds of gifts are mentioned in verses 8–10? How is each of these needed in a healthy church?

5. What do you see as the most important point this passage is making for your own church?

   ○ The same Lord unites us (v. 5).
   ○ I don't have to be like everyone else to belong here (vv. 14–17).
   ○ We all need each other (vv. 19–21).
   ○ We should all share in each other's suffering and rejoicing (v. 26).
   ○ Other _____.

6. When have you had the experience in a church of feeling like people were saying, "I don't need you"? How did you react?

7. Is it easy or difficult for you to believe that God has given you valuable gifts whereby you can contribute? What would you say is your most helpful gift when it comes to service to people in God's name?

Going Deeper If your group has time and/or wants a challenge, go on to this question.

8. How can the church better identify people's gifts and encourage people to use them in service to God?

 Caring Time Apply the Lesson and Pray for One Another **(15 minutes)**

For us to be able to find and use our gifts we need more than study—we need support and encouragement. This is your time to give that to each other. Share your responses to the following questions before closing in prayer.

1. What do you look forward to most about these meetings?

2. What honors or celebrations would you like the others in the group to join you in celebrating?

3. What is causing you suffering right now and how could the group support you?

Leader
Have you identified someone in the group that could be a leader for a new small group when your group divides? How could you encourage and mentor that person?

NEXT WEEK *Today we discussed spiritual gifts and how they can be used to bring people together in service to God. We were reminded that we each have something to contribute in helping to build up the body of Christ. In the coming week, take some time to evaluate how you are using your gifts for the kingdom of God. Next week we will focus on the greatest gift of all, the gift of love, and how it can be fostered in our relationships.*

Summary: Paul deals with unity within a church of diverse individuals. His emphasis in the first section (12:4–11) is on the variety of gifts given by the Spirit. Paul points out that not all Christians have the same gift (nor every gift), nor do they render the same service. However, all gifts spring from the same Spirit, are used to serve the same Lord, and are all energized by the power of the same God. Having pointed out the diversity of gifts, Paul then examines the unity that exists within all this diversity. After stating that Christians are all part of one body, Paul returns to the idea of diversity, in which he not only points out the variety of gifts that exist, but the fact that none are inferior and all are necessary

12:5 *ministries.* The purpose of the gifts is to serve and aid others in various ways, yet all is done in the name of and for the sake of the same Lord.

12:6 *activities.* The Greek root is *energeia* ("energy"), and refers to the various ways in which God's power is displayed in the gifts.

12:7 *to each person.* Every Christian has a spiritual gift. ***to produce what is beneficial.*** The purpose of these gifts is not private advantage, but community growth.

12:8 *through the Spirit.* Paul again emphasizes the supernatural origins of these gifts. ***wisdom/knowledge.*** It is not clear how (or if) these gifts differ. Perhaps a message of wisdom focused on practical, ethical instruction, while a message of knowledge involved exposition of biblical truth. In either case, the emphasis is on the actual discourse given for the benefit of the assembled Christians.

12:9 *faith.* This is the faith that Jesus said could "move mountains"—faith that God will act for the good of his children. Saving faith, which all Christians share, is not in view here. ***healing.*** Special ability to effect miraculous cures. Paul apparently had this gift (Acts 14:8–10).

12:10 *the performing of miracles.* Probably the gift of exorcism and similar types of confrontation with evil supernatural powers. ***prophecy.*** Inspired utterances given in ordinary speech, distinguished from teaching and wisdom by its unpremeditated nature. ***distinguishing between spirits.*** Just because a person claimed to be inspired by the Holy Spirit did not make it true. Those who possessed this gift of discernment were able to identify the source of an utterance—whether it came from the Holy Spirit or another spirit. ***different kinds of languages.*** Some interpret this to be ecstatic speech, unintelligible except by those with the gift of interpretation of tongues. Others believe it refers to the supernatural ability to speak in real, known languages (as apparently happened at Penteconst in Acts 2). ***interpretation of languages.*** This gift allowed a person to understand and explain to others what was being said by someone else in a tongue.

12:12 *is one and has many parts.* This is Paul's central point in verses 12–30: "diversity within unity." ***so also is Christ.*** The church is the body of Christ (v. 27), and so indeed Christ can be understood to be made up of many parts. Yet he is also the Lord (v. 3), and thus head over that church.

12:27 *the body of Christ.* By this phrase, Paul conveys the idea not that Christ consists of this body, but that Christ rules over this body, and that this body belongs to him.

12:28 Paul offers a second list of the types of gifts given by the Holy Spirit (see the parallel list in Eph. 4:11)—mixing together ministries (e.g., apostles) with spiritual gifts (e.g., the gift of healing). *apostles.* These individuals were responsible for founding new churches. They were pioneer church planters. *prophets.* Those who were inspired to speak God's word to the church, in plain language. *teachers.* Those gifted to instruct others in the meaning of the Christian faith and its implications for one's life. *next.* Having first focused on those gifts whereby the church is established and nurtured, Paul then shifts to other gifts. *helping.* The gift of support; those whose function it was to aid the needy (e.g., the poor, the widow, the orphan). *managing.* The gift of direction (literally, the process of steering a ship through the rocks and safely to shore); those whose function it was to guide church affairs.

12:31 *the greater gifts.* These are the gifts that edify the church most. In chapter 13 Paul establishes the context within which all gifts should function: love, which is the more excellent way.

Love

Scripture 1 Corinthians 12:31b–13:13

LAST WEEK *In last week's session, we focused on the spiritual gifts that each believer is given for the purposes of building up the body of Christ and furthering God's kingdom. We were reminded that each of the gifts is equally important, and the same Holy Spirit is active in each one. This week we will consider how love is the greatest of all the gifts of the Spirit.*

Ice-Breaker Connect With Your Group (15 minutes)

Paul says in today's Scripture passage that if he doesn't have love he is like a "sounding gong or a clanging cymbal." Take turns sharing your experiences with making a joyful noise or speaking a beautiful language.

Leader
Choose one or two of the Ice-Breaker questions. If you have a new group member, you may want to do all three. Remember to stick closely to the three-part agenda and the time allowed for each segment.

1. What musical instrument did you learn to play as a child or adolescent? How did those in your home tolerate those early (sometimes trying) times of listening to you practice? If you did not learn an instrument, what instrument would you have liked to learn?

2. What discordant or obnoxious noise irritates you the most?

   ○ Fingernails on a blackboard.
   ○ A screechy violin.
   ○ That noise you get over the phone when you dial a fax number by mistake?
   ○ A crying baby.
   ○ A clanging alarm clock.
   ○ Other _____.

3. What sound in nature is most soothing to you? What is it about that sound that makes you relax?

Bible Study Read Scripture and Discuss **(30 minutes)**

Love

Reader One: And I will show you an even better way.

13 If I speak the languages of men and of angels, but do not have love,

I am a sounding gong or a clanging cymbal.

²If I have the gift of prophecy,

and understand all mysteries and all knowledge,

and if I have all faith, so that I can move mountains,

but do not have love,

I am nothing.

³And if I donate all my goods to feed the poor,

and if I give my body to be burned,

but do not have love,

I gain nothing.

⁴Love is patient; love is kind. Love does not envy;

is not boastful; is not conceited;

⁵does not act improperly; is not selfish;

is not provoked; does not keep a record of wrongs;

⁶finds no joy in unrighteousness, but rejoices in the truth;

⁷bears all things, believes all things,

hopes all things, endures all things.

Reader Two: ⁸Love never ends.

But as for prophecies, they will come to an end;

as for languages, they will cease;

as for knowledge, it will come to an end.

⁹For we know in part, and we prophesy in part.

¹⁰But when the perfect comes, the partial will come to an end.

¹¹When I was a child, I spoke like a child I thought like a child, I reasoned like a child.

When I became a man, I put aside childish things.

¹²For now we see indistinctly, as in a mirror, but then face to face.

Now I know in part, but then I will know fully, as I am fully known.

¹³Now these three remain: faith, hope, and love.

But the greatest of these is love.

1 Corinthians 12:31b–13:13

Leader
Select two members of the group ahead of time to read aloud the Scripture passage. Have one person read 12:31b–13:7, and the other read 13:8–13. Then discuss the Questions for Interaction, dividing into subgroups of three to six.

Questions for Interaction

Leader
Refer to the Summary and Study Notes at the end of this session as needed. If 30 minutes is not enough time to answer all of the questions in this section, conclude the Bible Study by answering question 7.

1. When you were a child, what person most embodied love to you? What did this person do that was especially loving?

2. Paul refers to speaking in the languages of men and angels, prophesying, having great faith, feeding the poor and being a martyr to contrast the awesomeness of having God's love in our life. Why are these gifts ineffective without love?

3. How is God's love described in verses 4–8a? How is this love different from human love?

4. Why does Paul say that even with the benefits of the gifts found in verse 2 he is "nothing"?

5. What is meant by "when the perfect comes" (v. 10)? What will we "know fully" in the future (v. 12)?

6. What does God's love mean to you? Have you ever experienced this kind of love in a relationship?

7. Which of these phrases from verses 4–5 will you focus on in your life this week, and why?

   ○ **Love is patient:** I won't take out my frustrations on those I love. I will be calm under pressure and careful with my tongue.
   ○ **Love is kind:** I will go out of my way to say nice words and do thoughtful things for others.
   ○ **Love does not envy:** I won't be envious of others' gifts and abilities or of what they have. Neither will I be jealous with my time toward those who need me.
   ○ **Love is not boastful:** I won't consider my role any more important than those I love—or talk like "I know better."
   ○ **Love does not act improperly:** I won't make cutting or crude remarks when I don't get my own way—or become silent and withdrawn.
   ○ **Love is not selfish:** I won't put myself first. I will try to give those I love spiritual and emotional support.
   ○ **Love is not provoked:** I won't let little things bother me, especially with those I love. I will have a muffler on my mouth.
   ○ **Love does not keep a record of wrongs:** I won't keep score of the number of times those I love say something or do something to upset me, and I won't bring it up when we have a conflict or disagreement.

8. How does love as described in this chapter compare to love as typically defined in our culture?

Caring Time Apply the Lesson and Pray for One Another (15 minutes)

Gather around each other now in this time of sharing and prayer, and help each member to experience God's love. Begin by sharing your responses to the following questions. Then take some time to share prayer requests and pray for one another.

1. Based on this description of love in chapter 13, how would your family and friends rate your "love meter" this last week, on a scale of 1 (barely registering) to 10 (off the scale)?

2. Who in your life needs to receive God's love from you this week? How will you express it?

3. How can this group pray for you regarding your answer to question 7?

Leader
Conclude the prayer time today by reading 1 John 4:10–12: *Love consists in this: not that we loved God, but that He loved us and sent His Son to be the propitiation for our sins. Dear friends, if God loved us in this way, we also must love one another. No one has ever seen God. If we love one another, God remains in us and His love is perfected in us.*

NEXT WEEK *Today we discussed the power of God's love and how important it is for us to develop this in our lives. We were reminded that love should be the motivating factor behind all that we do. In the coming week, follow through on your answer to question 2 in the Caring Time, and spread God's love to one another. Next week we will consider two other gifts that have had importance to the church and were at the center of a dispute in Corinth—prophecy and speaking in tongues. We will also look at worship and the use of gifts in worship.*

Summary: If a person does not love, neither spiritual gifts, nor good deeds, nor martyrdom is of any ultimate value to that person. Love is the context within which these gifts and deeds become significant.

13:1 *languages of men and of angels.* Speaking in tongues (highly prized in Corinth) is an authentic gift of the Holy Spirit. However, it becomes like the unintelligible noise of pagan worship when used outside the context of love. *gong/cymbal.* Paul is probably thinking of the repetitive and meaningless noise generated at pagan temples by beating on metal instruments.

13:2 Paul contrasts three other spiritual gifts with love: prophecy, knowledge and faith. *prophecy.* Such activity is highly commended by Paul (14:1), yet without love a prophet is really nothing. *understand all mysteries.* Even if one knew the very secrets of God, without love it would be to no end. That which makes a person significant (i.e., the opposite of "nothing") is not a gift like prophecy or knowledge, but the ability to love. *faith, so that I can move mountains.* Paul refers to Jesus' words in Mark 11:23—even such massive faith that can unleash God's power in visible ways is not enough to make a person significant without love at its foundation.

13:3 *donate all my goods to feed the poor.* Presumably Paul refers to goods and property given to others, but not in love. The poor still profit from gifts, regardless of the spirit in which they are given, but the loveless giver gains no reward on the Day of Judgment. *give my body.* Not even martyrdom—giving up one's life for the sake of another or in a great cause—brings personal benefit when it is done outside love.

13:4 *patient.* This word describes patience with people (not circumstances). It characterizes the person who is slow to anger (long-suffering) despite provocation. *kind.* The loving person does good to others. *does not envy.* The loving person does not covet what others have, nor begrudge them their possessions. *not boastful.* The loving person is self-effacing, not a braggart. *not conceited.* Literally, not "puffed up." The loving person does not feel others to be inferior, nor look down on people.

13:5 *does not act improperly.* The same Greek word is used in 1 Corinthians 7:36 to describe a man who led on a woman, but then refused to marry her. *not selfish.* Loving people not only do not insist on their rights, but will give up their due for the sake of others. *not provoked.* Others do not easily anger loving people; they are not touchy. *does not keep a record of wrongs.* The verb is an accounting term, and the image is of a ledger sheet on which wrongs received are recorded. The loving person forgives and forgets.

13:6 *finds no joy in unrighteousness.* Loving people do not rejoice when others fail (which could make them feel superior), nor enjoy pointing out the wrong in others. *rejoices in the truth.* Paul shifts back to the positive.

13:7 *bears all things.* Literally, "to put a cover over." The loving person is concerned with how to shelter other people from harm. *believes all things.* The loving person never loses faith. *hopes all things.* Love continually looks forward. *endures all things.* Love keeps loving despite hardship.

13:8 *Love never ends.* In the sense that it functions both now and in the age to come. Spiritual gifts are relevant only to this age. ***come to an end/cease.*** One day, when Christ comes again in fullness, prophecy will be fulfilled (and come to an end), the indirect communication with God through tongues will no longer be needed (so they cease), and since all will be revealed and be evident, secret knowledge about God will be redundant (and come to an end). Each of these are partial revelations about God, vital in this present age, but unnecessary in the age to come.

13:11 The contrast is between this age (when we are still children) and the age to come (when we will be mature).

13:12 ***now/then.*** Paul is thinking of the Second Coming. The here-and-now experience is contrasted to the time when Christ's kingdom will be revealed in its fullness. ***indistinctly.*** Corinth was famous for the mirrors it made out of highly polished metal. Still, no mirror manufactured in the first century was without imperfections. All of them distorted the image somewhat, and so this is an apt metaphor for the present knowledge of God—it is marred (until the day we see the Lord clearly in heaven).

13:13 ***remain.*** Charismatic gifts will cease, because they bring only partial knowledge of God; but three things will carry over into the new age: faith, hope and love. ***the greatest of these is love.*** Love is the greatest gift because God is love (1 John 4:8). After everything else is no longer necessary, love will still be the governing principle.

Gifts and Worship

Scripture 1 Corinthians 14:1–12,26–33a

> **LAST WEEK** *"But the greatest of these is love" (13:13). Last week we focused on love—the greatest of all the gifts of the Spirit. We were reminded that everything we do should be motivated by love: otherwise it has no meaning. This week we will consider two other spiritual gifts that caused some controversy in the Corinthian church and can still cause controversy today—prophecy and other languages (ecstatic and foreign languages). We will also look at worship and the use of gifts in worship.*

 Ice-Breaker Connect With Your Group (15 minutes)

Prophesying and speaking in tongues are spiritual gifts that many of us never see or experience. But we do like to think about and plan for the future, and sometimes we even try to communicate with others who speak a different language. Take turns sharing some of your experiences in these areas.

Leader
Open with a word of prayer. Choose one, two or all three Ice-Breaker questions, depending on your group's needs.

1. If the kids with whom you grew up could have prophesied a future for you, which of the following would they have been most likely to prophesy?

   ○ Most likely to succeed.
   ○ Most likely to end up in "the slammer."
   ○ Most likely to end up on the stage.
   ○ Destined to a life of flipping hamburgers.
   ○ Destined to a life of unrequited love.
   ○ Destined to change the world.
   ○ Other _____.

2. When have you been in a country or area when you couldn't speak the language? How did you feel at the time? What did you learn in the process?

3. When do you have the greatest need for an "interpreter"?

○ When I'm trying to get something across to my kids.
○ When I'm trying to get something across to my spouse.
○ When I'm with a group of teenagers and they are using their lingo.
○ When I'm trying to read a government document.
○ When I'm trying to read the "easy instructions" on a new electronic product.
○ Other _____.

 Bible Study Read Scripture and Discuss (30 minutes)

Most international airports today have multiple languages going out over the echoing intercoms. It can be quite noisy and confusing at times. Paul here writes about the confusion spiritual languages can bring to the church and, as a result, make worship chaotic instead of orderly. Read 1 Corinthians 14:1–12,26–33a and note how spiritual gifts and worship should always build up the church.

Leader
Select three members of the group ahead of time to read aloud the Scripture passage. Have the first member read verses 1–5; another read verses 6–12; and the third person read verses 26–33a. Then discuss the Questions for Interaction, dividing into subgroups of three to six.

Gifts and Worship

Reader One: 14 Pursue love and desire spiritual gifts, and above all that you may prophesy. [2]For the person who speaks in another language is not speaking to men but to God, since no one understands him; however, he speaks mysteries in the Spirit. [3]But the person who prophesies speaks to people for edification, encouragement, and consolation. [4]The person who speaks in another language builds himself up, but he who prophesies builds up the church. [5]I wish all of you spoke in other languages, but even more that you prophesied. The person who prophesies is greater than the person who speaks in languages, unless he interprets so that the church may be built up.

Reader Two: [6]But now, brothers, if I come to you speaking in other languages, how will I benefit you unless I speak to you with a revelation or knowledge or prophecy or teaching? [7]Even inanimate things producing sounds—whether flute or harp—if they don't make a distinction in the notes, how will what is played on the flute or harp be recognized? [8]In fact, if the trumpet makes an unclear sound, who will prepare for battle? [9]In the same way, unless you use your tongue for intelligible speech, how will what is spoken be known? For you will be speaking into the air. [10]There are doubtless many different kinds of languages in the world, and all have meaning. [11]Therefore, if I do not know the meaning of the language, I will be a foreigner to the

74

speaker, and the speaker will be a foreigner to me. [12]So also you—since you are zealous in matters of the spirit, seek to excel in building up the church.

Reader Three: [26]How is it then, brothers? Whenever you come together, each one has a psalm, a teaching, a revelation, another language, or an interpretation. All things must be done for edification. [27]If any person speaks in another language, there should be only two, or at the most three, each in turn, and someone must interpret. [28]But if there is no interpreter, that person should keep silent in the church and speak to himself and to God. [29]Two or three prophets should speak, and the others should evaluate. [30]But if something has been revealed to another person sitting there, the first prophet should be silent. [31]For you can all prophesy one by one, so that everyone may learn and everyone may be encouraged. [32]And the prophets' spirits are under the control of the prophets, [33]since God is not a God of disorder but of peace.

1 Corinthians 14:1–12,26–33a

Questions for Interaction

Leader
Refer to the Summary and Study Notes at the end of this session as needed. If 30 minutes is not enough time to answer all of the questions in this section, conclude the Bible Study by answering question 7.

1. What was the most inspiring part of the worship service you attended most recently?

   ○ The sermon.
   ○ A prayer.
   ○ The music.
   ○ A greeting from someone.
   ○ Other _____.

2. What is the difference between speaking in "other languages" and prophesying, and in what sense is prophecy better than speaking in "other languages" (vv. 2–5)?

3. What is the point of the musical allusions Paul is making in verses 6–9? What does this say about the weakness of the gift of tongues or speaking in other languages?

4. In what ways did people contribute to worship in the early church (v. 26)? Does worship in your church offer meaningful ways to participate instead of merely observing?

5. How do you feel about the use of the gifts of other languages and interpretation and prophecy today? By what standards should followers of Christ "evaluate" what is said (v. 29)?

6. Verse 33 says, "God is not a God of disorder but of peace." What does this characteristic of God mean to you?

7. In what ways are you using the gifts you have been given "in building up the church" (v. 12)? Are you "excelling" in this area or just getting by?

Going Deeper If your group has time and/or wants a challenge, go on to this question.

8. Is there one set way for a church to worship? If your church were to study this passage together and truly take it seriously, how would it change the way you worship?

 Caring Time Apply the Lesson and Pray for One Another (15 minutes)

Rejoice in the work of the Holy Spirit in your group, and join in a time of sharing and prayer. After responding to the following questions, share prayer requests and close with a group prayer.

Leader
Conclude the prayer time today by asking God for guidance in determining the future mission and outreach of this group.

1. How have you seen the Holy Spirit at work in your life this past week?

2. Where do you need to bring peace out of disorder in your life?

3. In what ways can this group better use their gifts to build each other up? Pray that God will help you to do this.

NEXT WEEK *Today we finished our discussion of spiritual gifts by seeing how they are used in worship. We were reminded that all gifts are to be used to build up the body of Christ, and that they should bring order and not chaos to our worship. In the coming week, ask the Holy Spirit to show you how your worship could be more meaningful to you and helpful to your fellow worshipers. Next week we will consider Christ's resurrection and the centrality of that resurrection to the Christian faith.*

Summary: Paul attacks head-on the problem they are experiencing with the gift of other languages (ecstatic or foreign languages): during their worship services, far too much time was spent speaking in tongues. The result was that chaos, not order, prevailed. In these verses, Paul contrasts gifts that are intelligible and which edify the community (such as prophecy) with gifts that are unintelligible and which edify only the individual (such as tongues). By using this series of contrasts, Paul shows why prophecy is to be preferred over tongues. Paul concludes his thoughts (begun in 11:2) by outlining quite specifically how certain spiritual gifts are to be used when the church assembles together—his main point being that when it comes to worship, order—not disorder—is the way of God.

14:1 Paul defines the theme of chapter 14 by means of three imperatives that are to be followed in this order: First, "pursue love"; second, in that context, "desire spiritual gifts"; and third, in your eager desire for gifts which has love as its aim, desire "above all that you may prophesy." The Corinthians had precisely the opposite order. **Pursue.** It is virtually synonymous with the next verb: "desire." **love.** As defined in chapter 13, love is the primary calling for all Christians and the context within which spiritual gifts are to be used.

14:2 Paul's first point about tongues is that, while they may be intelligible to God (who, after all, is the source of languages), they are not intelligible to other people.

14:3 In contrast, prophecy is intelligible and brings three benefits to the congregation: it builds them up, it encourages and it comforts. **prophesies.** This is not so much future prediction as it is moral exhortation and theological instruction—probably as related to particular problems and issues being faced by the community.

14:4 In the second contrast, Paul points out who is edified by each gift: while tongues edify the individual (and there is no hint that this is not of great value), prophecy edifies many (and the way of love would therefore give this gift primary emphasis).

14:5 While affirming the value of both other languages and prophecy, Paul stresses prophecy because of its value during the worship service. **languages.** In verses 2–5, Paul gives insight into just what languages are. They seem to be a gift from the Holy Spirit whereby an individual "speaks mysteries" to God by (or in) the Spirit, from which great personal benefit is gained. Un-interpreted languages, however, are meant to be part of private devotions, not public worship. **greater.** In the sense that prophecy edifies, and is therefore an act of love. Interpreted languages have the same use and value as prophecy.

14:6 *revelation/knowledge/prophecy/teaching.* These four gifts all deal with forms of Christian instruction. It is difficult to distinguish sharply between them. The differences may be in the content of the instruction: revelation dealing with hidden aspects of God's truth (Rom. 16:25; 2 Cor. 12:1,7); knowledge as exposition of revealed truth; prophecy as insight from God into a specific situation; and a word of instruction (literally, "teaching") as the general application of Christian truth.

14:7 The point of playing an instrument is not just to make sounds, but also to play a recognizable tune.

14:8 A trumpet can be used to alert an army for battle, but if the wrong note (or a weak note) is sounded, the soldiers will be unclear as to what is expected of them. It will be merely noise to them.

14:9 *speaking into the air.* This is what tongues are from the standpoint of the hearer—mere random sound.

14:10–11 While each language has meaning, when spoken to a foreigner, this language is just gibberish—the one speaking might as well have said absolutely nothing.

14:11 *foreigner.* The Greek word is *barbaros* (barbarian). Foreigners were so named because to cultured Greek ears, their languages sounded like gibberish, as if they were saying, "brrbrr."

14:26 Paul reiterates that each believer has a gift to offer during worship, that there are a variety of gifts and they are to be used to edify. Worship was not an event where only a few were active and one person preached a sermon. All were an active part. *a psalm.* Singing is a gift. The reference here may be to "singing in the Spirit" (14:15). ***All things.*** Probably a representative list of the sort of gifts used during worship. The list is not exhaustive because it does not include, for example, prophecy or discernment of spirits (previously mentioned in the context of worship, and assumed in the verses that follow).

14:29 *evaluate.* Simply because a prophecy is uttered does not make it automatically true. Not only does its "source" have to be noted by those gifted in such discernment (12:10), but also the whole body must carefully consider its content (12:3; 1 Thess. 5:20–21).

14:30 ***something has been revealed.*** This might be some type of pressing vision, the content of which must be shared right away before it passes.

Resurrection

Scripture 1 Corinthians 15:1–28

LAST WEEK *In last week's session, we focused on how our spiritual gifts should be used in worship. Paul especially addressed chaos and division within the Corinthian church. We were reminded that every spiritual gift should be used to build up the body of Christ. This week we will look at a hope that is at the core of our faith—the hope of resurrection through Jesus Christ.*

 Ice-Breaker Connect With Your Group (15 minutes)

We all love a great story, especially if it's true. Today we will hear Paul tell the story of Jesus and the glorious future that is awaiting each believer. Take turns sharing your thoughts and experiences with storytelling.

Leader
Open with a word of prayer, and then have your group discuss one, two or all three of the Ice-Breaker questions.

1. What stories do you remember your parents and/or grandparents telling you about things that were important to your family history? How do you feel about having such "roots"?

2. What funny story about your childhood do you especially remember?

3. Who do you remember first telling you the very basic story of what the Gospel was all about?

 Bible Study Read Scripture and Discuss (30 minutes)

Life is precious. We only need to have one near brush with death to realize how fragile life can be. As followers of Christ, we have a hope that others cannot have without Christ. This is a confident hope that assures us we will "stay alive" forever. The sole reason for that is the resurrection of our Lord and his victory over the grave. Read 1 Corinthians 15:1–28 and note how Paul points out that without belief in the Resurrection our faith would be "useless."

Leader
Select a member of the group ahead of time to read aloud the Scripture passage. Then discuss the Questions for Interaction, dividing into subgroups of three to six.

Resurrection

15 Now brothers, I want to clarify for you the gospel I proclaimed to you; you received it and have taken your stand on it. [2]You are also saved by it, if you hold to the message I proclaimed to you—unless you believed to no purpose. [3]For I passed on to you as most important what I also received:

> that Christ died for our sins according to the Scriptures,
> [4]that He was buried,
> that He was raised on the third day according to the Scriptures,
> [5]and that He appeared to Cephas, then to the Twelve.
> [6]Then He appeared to over 500 brothers at one time,
> most of whom remain to the present, but some have fallen asleep.
> [7]Then He appeared to James, then to all the apostles.
> [8]Last of all, as to one abnormally born, He also appeared to me.

[9]For I am the least of the apostles, unworthy to be called an apostle, because I persecuted the church of God. [10]But by God's grace I am what I am, and His grace toward me was not ineffective. However, I worked more than any of them, yet not I, but God's grace that was with me. [11]Therefore, whether it is I or they, so we preach and so you have believed.

[12]Now if Christ is preached as raised from the dead, how can some of you say, "There is no resurrection of the dead"? [13]But if there is no resurrection of the dead, then Christ has not been raised; [14]and if Christ has not been raised, then our preaching is without foundation, and so is your faith. [15]In addition, we are found to be false witnesses about God, because we have testified about God that He raised up Christ—whom He did not raise up if in fact the dead are not raised. [16]For if the dead are not raised, Christ has not been raised. [17]And if Christ has not been raised, your faith is worthless; you are still in your sins. [18]Therefore those who have fallen asleep in Christ have also perished. [19]If we have placed our hope in Christ for this life only, we should be pitied more than anyone.

[20]But now Christ has been raised from the dead, the firstfruits of those who have fallen asleep. [21]For since death came through a man, the resurrection of the dead also comes through a man. [22]For just as in Adam all die, so also in Christ all will be made alive. [23]But each in his own order: Christ, the firstfruits; afterward, at His coming, the people of Christ. [24]Then comes the end, when He hands over the kingdom to God the Father, when He abolishes all rule and all authority and power. [25]For He must reign until He puts all His enemies under His feet. [26]The last enemy He abolishes is death. [27]For He has put everything under His feet. But when it says "everything" is put under Him, it is obvious that He who puts everything under Him is the exception. [28]And when everything is subject to Him, then the Son Himself will also be subject to Him who subjected everything to Him, so that God may be all in all.

1 Corinthians 15:1–28

Questions for Interaction

Leader
Refer to the Summary and Study Notes at the end of this session as needed. If 30 minutes is not enough time to answer all of the questions in this section, conclude the Bible Study by answering question 7.

1. When do you remember having to "take a stand" as a teenager or young adult, and how difficult was it?

   ○ When I didn't want to go along with the crowd and smoke or drink.
   ○ When I was criticized for my faith.
   ○ When I stood up for a friend who was being threatened.
   ○ When I debated politics with my friends.
   ○ Other _____.

2. In reminding the Corinthians about the Gospel, Paul says they had taken their "stand on it" (v. 1). How had the Corinthians taken their stand on the Gospel?

3. What are the main points of the Gospel Paul received and passed on to the Corinthians (vv. 3–8)?

4. What false teaching was being accepted by some in the Corinthian church (v. 12)? Why does this kind of cynicism keep showing up, even in the church today?

5. According to Paul, in what way does all of the Christian faith rest upon the reality of resurrection from the dead? Why does he say that if it is not true, Christians are to be pitied even more than others (see note on vv. 17–19)?

6. Why is it important that death itself will one day be destroyed (vv. 26–28)? What difference has Christ's resurrection and your resulting victory over death made to you in terms of hope and courage? In terms of purpose for life?

7. When have you had to confront your own mortality in more than merely an intellectual way?

   ○ When I was told I had a serious health problem.
   ○ When I mourned the death of a loved one.
   ○ When I witnessed an accident or community tragedy.
   ○ When I went through the emotions of a catastrophic event, such as 9/11/01.
   ○ Other _____.

Did this make you feel differently about your faith in the Resurrection? In what way?

If your group has time and/or wants a challenge, go on to this question.

8. Given what Paul says here, how would you explain the importance of the Resurrection to a non-Christian?

 Caring Time Apply the Lesson and Pray for One Another (15 minutes)

Come together now and encourage one another with the hope that Jesus has given us through his death and resurrection. Begin by sharing your responses to the following questions. Then share prayer requests and close in a group prayer.

1. What can you do in the coming week to encourage someone who has lost hope?

2. What "scars" do you still have from the loss of a loved one to death? How can the group pray for you for healing from this loss?

3. How can this group be supportive of you in regard to your anxieties about your own mortality? Are there present health problems we should be praying about?

Leader
Following the Caring Time, discuss with your group how they would like to celebrate the last session next week. Also, discuss the possibility of splitting into two groups and continuing with another study.

NEXT WEEK *Today Paul summarized for us what the Christian faith is all about. He reminded us that our hope is in the death and resurrection of Jesus, and that some day we will have victory over death. In the coming week, take some time to think about heaven and all that you have to look forward to when you are resurrected. Next week we will finish our study of 1 Corinthians by considering what our resurrection body will be like.*

Summary: In chapter 15 Paul turns to a theological problem, in contrast to the largely behavioral problems he has dealt with thus far. Some Corinthians are denying that in the future believers will be raised from the dead. The problem may be simply one of ignorance, because no one instructed them in this matter. (The Thessalonians, for example, did not know about the resurrection of the dead, as Paul says in 1 Thess. 4:13–18.) Paul begins this chapter by pointing to something the Corinthians believed: that Christ rose from the dead. Christ's resurrection is the key to Paul's argument that believers will also be resurrected.

15:1 *gospel.* Literally, "good news"; a term used in Greek literature to signify a positive event of great significance (for example, the birth of a future emperor or the winning of an important battle). It is used by Paul (and others in the New Testament) to designate the core message of Christianity—that in Jesus Christ God fulfilled his promises and opened a way of salvation to all people. In the next few verses, Paul will define the content of this message.

15:3–4 This is the earliest written definition of the "Gospel." It consists of three statements of historical fact (Christ died, was buried and rose again), and two words of explanation—he died "for our sins" (i.e., to deal with them), and all this is "according to the Scriptures" (i.e., a fulfillment of God's plan).

15:3 *what I also received.* Paul did not make up the Gospel. It was common to the church. He simply passed on what he had been given. *for our sins.* When Christ died, it was in order to deal with the fact of our sin. By his death as a substitute in our place, Christ enabled men and women to be forgiven for their sins, to come back into relationship with God, and to have new life. *according to the Scriptures.* Christ's death fulfilled the prophecies found in Old Testament Scripture (Isa. 52:13–53:12).

15:4 *He was buried.* Jesus was really dead, and so he really rose from the dead. It was a real resurrection, not just resuscitation. *He was raised.*

Paul shifts the tense of the verb (in Greek) from the aorist tense (completed past action—"died/buried") to the perfect tense, with the idea that what once happened is even now still in force.

15:5 *He appeared.* Paul's emphasis in this statement of the Gospel is on Jesus' resurrection (because of the argument he is building in chapter 15), so here he points to six post-resurrection appearances, each of which substantiate that Christ indeed rose (Matt. 28:16–20; Mark 16:7; Luke 24:31–51; John 20:19–23).

15:6 *to over 500 brothers ... most of whom remain to the present.* Paul is inviting people to check out for themselves the reality of Christ's resurrection. Those who witnessed the resurrected Christ were still alive. This is a strong proof of Christ's resurrection, because in this public letter Paul would never have challenged people in this way if these witnesses had not, indeed, seen the resurrected Christ and could therefore be counted upon to verify this fact.

15:7 *to James.* This appearance is not recorded, but James was widely respected as the leader of the church in Jerusalem. *to all the apostles.* For example, in Acts 1:6–11.

15:8 *Last of all.* This appearance came several years after the resurrection of Christ (Acts

9:1–8). **abnormally born.** This probably refers to the fact that, unlike Peter and James, circumstances were such that Paul never knew Jesus during his earthly ministry.

15:12 Now. Having established the fact of Christ's resurrection (vv. 3–8), Paul now pushes the argument forward: Jesus' resurrection is a clear proof that there is such a thing as resurrection. **how can some of you say.** Now Paul pinpoints directly the false teaching against which he is contending.

15:14 our preaching/your faith. The Corinthians owe their very existence as a church to these two things: Paul's preaching and their response of faith. Central to both the preaching and their faith is the resurrection of Christ. And since the church does indeed exist, this is another proof of Christ's resurrection.

15:16 if the dead are not raised. This is the first of three times in this section (vv. 12–34) that Paul uses this phrase that summarizes the implications of their errant view about the resurrection of the body. If the dead are not raised, then: (a) Christ could not have been resurrected (and they believe that he was), (b) there would be no point in baptizing people for the dead (as they were apparently doing—v. 29), and (c) believers might as well "live it up," since they had no future (v. 32).

15:20 But now Christ has been raised. Having sketched the horror of no resurrection, Paul relieves the gloom and shifts to this positive affirmation. This is the essential declaration, without which there is no Christianity. **firstfruits.** The early developing grains or fruits that demonstrate the full harvest is not far behind. Similarly, the fact that Christ was raised from the dead is clear proof that the future resurrection of believers is assured.

15:22 Adam. Adam sinned, and so death entered into the world (Gen. 2:17). Thus all people since that time experience death (Rom. 5:12–21). **all will be made alive.** Though the wording has been made parallel to the previous clause ("all die"), the idea is that all who are in Christ will rise, as Paul says explicitly in 1 Thessalonians 4:16–17.

The Resurrection Body

Scripture 1 Corinthians 15:35–58

LAST WEEK *The hope we have because of the death and resurrection of Jesus Christ was our focus in last week's session. We were reminded that without the Resurrection, we would be lost in our sins and our faith would be worthless. This week, in our final session, we will delve into this subject even more as we look at the nature of the resurrection body and the glorious future that awaits each believer.*

Ice-Breaker Connect With Your Group (15 minutes)

When we look at the stars it's hard for our minds to comprehend how many there are and the beauty of what we're seeing. Paul has us try to comprehend something equally as awesome in today's Scripture reading, when he shares that our natural body is like a seed, and out of it will grow a "spiritual body" that is incorruptible. Take turns sharing some of your thoughts about seeds, your body and stargazing.

Leader
Begin this final session with a word of prayer and thanksgiving for this time together. Choose one or two Ice-Breaker questions to discuss.

1. What kind of seed have you been most likely to plant in your lifetime?

   ○ Garden seeds—I have a green thumb.
   ○ Seeds of discontent—I'm a troublemaker from way back.
   ○ Seeds of hope—I'm always looking for the positive.
   ○ Seeds of change—I'm always disrupting the status quo.
   ○ Other _____.

2. What do you like about your body? What would you most like to change?

3. When is the last time you remember going out stargazing? How did you feel at the time? What keeps you from doing it more often?

Bible Study Read Scripture and Discuss (30 minutes)

As Paul concludes this book, he challenges us to think about eternity. Because of Christ we have victory over death and we can focus our lives on making an impact for the kingdom of God. Read 1 Corinthians 15:35–58 and note the glory and power that will be ours if we press on in this life.

Leader

Select two members of the group ahead of time to read aloud the Scripture passage. Have one member read verses 35–49, and the other read verses 50–58. Then discuss the Questions for Interaction, dividing into subgroups of three to six. Be sure to save some extra time at the end for the Caring Time.

The Resurrection Body

Reader One: ³⁵But someone will say, "How are the dead raised? What kind of body will they have when they come?" ³⁶Foolish one! What you sow does not come to life unless it dies. ³⁷And as for what you sow—you are not sowing the future body, but only a seed, perhaps of wheat or another grain. ³⁸But God gives it a body as He wants, and to each of the seeds its own body. ³⁹Not all flesh is the same flesh; there is one flesh for humans, another for animals, another for birds, and another for fish. ⁴⁰There are heavenly bodies and earthly bodies, but the splendor of the heavenly bodies is different from that of the earthly ones. ⁴¹There is a splendor of the sun, another of the moon, and another of the stars; for star differs from star in splendor. ⁴²So it is with the resurrection of the dead:

Sown in corruption, raised in incorruption;
⁴³sown in dishonor, raised in glory;
sown in weakness, raised in power;
⁴⁴sown a natural body, raised a spiritual body.

If there is a natural body, there is also a spiritual body. ⁴⁵So it is written: The first man Adam became a living being; the last Adam became a life-giving Spirit. ⁴⁶However, the spiritual is not first, but the natural; then the spiritual.

⁴⁷The first man was from the earth and made of dust;
the second man is from heaven.
⁴⁸Like the man made of dust, so are those who are made of dust;
like the heavenly man, so are those who are heavenly.
⁴⁹And just as we have borne the image of the man made of dust,
we will also bear the image of the heavenly man.

Reader Two: ⁵⁰Brothers, I tell you this: flesh and blood cannot inherit the kingdom of God, and corruption cannot inherit incorruption. ⁵¹Listen! I am telling you a mystery:

We will not all fall asleep, but we will all be changed,
⁵²in a moment, in the twinkling of an eye, at the last trumpet.

For the trumpet will sound, and the dead will be raised incorruptible,
and we will be changed.
[53]Because this corruptible must be clothed with incorruptibility,
and this mortal must be clothed with immortality.
[54]Now when this corruptible is clothed with incorruptibility,
and this mortal is clothed with immortality,
then the saying that is written will take place:
Death has been swallowed up in victory.
[55]O Death, where is your victory?
O Death, where is your sting?
[56]Now the sting of death is sin, and the power of sin is the law.
[57]But thanks be to God, who gives us the victory
through our Lord Jesus Christ!

[58]Therefore, my dear brothers, be steadfast, immovable, always excelling in the Lord's work, knowing that your labor in the Lord is not in vain.

1 Corinthians 15:35–58

Questions for Interaction

Leader
Refer to the Summary and Study Notes at the end of this session as needed. If 30 minutes is not enough time to answer all of the questions in this section, conclude the Bible Study by answering question 7.

1. If you could have Jesus here in the flesh to answer just one of your questions about the nature of death and resurrection, what would it be?

2. How is dying like planting a seed, according to Paul? What is a seed like when it is planted? What is it like when it is grown? How is this like the connection between a physical body and a resurrection body?

3. What are the main differences that Paul points out between the physical body and the resurrection body (vv. 42–44)?

4. What does Paul mean by saying, "And just as we have borne the image of the man made of dust, we will also bear the image of the heavenly man" (v. 49)? Who is "the man made of dust"? Who is "the heavenly man"?

5. How have you experienced the "sting" of death?

6. How did Jesus take away the "sting" of death for us?

7. What is most comforting to you from these verses when you consider the reality of your own eventual death?

Going Deeper If your group has time and/or wants a challenge, go on to this question.

8. What does Paul mean by "The sting of death is sin" (v. 56)? How does the presence of sin make the reality of death tragic and painful?

 Caring Time Apply the Lesson and Pray for One Another (15 minutes)

Gather around each other now in this final time of sharing and prayer and encourage one another to have faith and hope as you go back out into the world.

Leader
Conclude this final Caring Time by praying for each group member and asking for God's blessing in any plans to start a new group and/or continue to study together.

1. What was your serendipity (unexpected blessing) during this course?

2. What was the high point for you in this study of 1 Corinthians? What will you take with you?

3. How would you like the group to continue to pray for you?

Summary: The false teachers in Corinth may be arguing against the future resurrection by asserting that it is absurd to imagine the resuscitation of an immense number of corpses. The question is "foolish" (v. 36) when put that way, especially since it misses the whole point of the resurrection, which is the transformation of the natural into the spiritual. Still, Paul must deal with the issue, and so the subject of verses 35–58 is the nature of the resurrection body. Paul concludes his argument for the resurrection of believers with a magnificent passage in which he points triumphantly to the future hope of the Christian.

15:36–38 Death brings change (transformation), not extinction. Here, Paul probes the nature of the transformation; his point being that what one plants (or buries) is not what one gets in the end. A small grain of wheat grows mysteriously into a tall, grain-bearing stalk (John 12:24). So, too, their bodies will yield new and glorious bodies after the resurrection.

15:39–41 A second analogy is used to show that there are a host of different kinds of bodies, and it is not unreasonable to expect the resurrection body to be quite different from the natural body.

15:42 *in corruption.* In other words, "perishable."

15:43 Paul now describes the nature of the changed body. The resurrection body is characterized by glory (brightness, radiance, splendor). This is a quality ascribed to God, in which believers will somehow share (Phil. 3:21). The resurrection body will also be filled with power—another word often used to describe Christ.

15:44 *natural/spiritual.* The natural body is that which is animated by the soul (i.e., the natural life force), while the spiritual body has as its animating force the Holy Spirit.

15:48 The Christians, after their resurrection, will become a race of heavenly people.

15:49 *the heavenly man.* This is Jesus, whose image Christians will reflect both in terms of character and glory.

15:50 *flesh and blood.* That is, living people cannot inherit the kingdom. ***corruption.*** Nor can the unchanged dead inherit the kingdom. What Paul is saying is that at the Second Coming neither the living nor the dead can take part in the kingdom without being changed.

15:51 *mystery.* A truth about the end times, once hidden but now revealed. ***We.*** Paul expected to be alive at the Second Coming. ***not all fall asleep.*** Some Christians will be alive at the Second Coming. ***all be changed.*** Both the living and the dead will be changed.

15:52 *in a moment.* This change will occur instantaneously. ***the trumpet will sound.*** The sounding of the trumpet was used to rally an army for action. This image is used to describe God's calling his people together (1 Thess. 4:16). ***the dead will be raised.*** Those who are in the grave at the Second Coming will be transformed, as will the living.

15:54 *the saying that is written will take place.* Paul cites two texts from the Old Testament—here (the quote is from Isa. 25:8) and in verse 55—which have yet to be fulfilled.

15:55 Death has been swallowed up in the victory of the resurrection. Using Hosea 13:14, Paul "taunts" death.

15:56 *the sting of death is sin.* Sin brings a sting to death because when we are in sin, death means judgment and destruction, instead of life eternal. ***the power of sin is the law.*** By this Paul means that the Law has the unfortunate result of arousing sin within people. As he shows from his own example in Romans 7, the Law's command not to covet did not deliver him from covetousness but actually stirred him up to feel it all the more.

15:57 *victory.* In great joy, Paul exults in the fact that sin and the Law (that by which sin is made known) do not have the last word. Christ's death was a victory over sin and death.

15:58 *be steadfast.* His letter is at an end; his chastening is finished, and so it is appropriate that he challenge them to allow this same Christ who has won victories for them to win victories through them. ***your labor in the Lord is not in vain.*** Because the resurrection is real, the future is secure and magnificent.

Individual and Group Needs Survey

Check the types of studies that you find most interesting:
- ❒ Issues about spiritual development, such as learning to love like God does or knowing God's will.
- ❒ Studying about the life and message of Jesus Christ.
- ❒ Issues about personal development, such as managing stress or understanding the stages of growth in marriage.
- ❒ Learning about the major truths of the Christian faith.
- ❒ Studying the teaching of the Apostle Paul.
- ❒ Working through specific areas of personal struggle, such as coping with teenagers or recovering from divorce.
- ❒ Learning about the books of the New Testament other than the Gospels and Epistles of Paul.

Rank the following factor in order of importance to you with 1 being the highest and five being the lowest:
- _____ The passage of Scripture that is being studied.
- _____ The topic or issue that is being discussed.
- _____ The affinity of group members (age, vocation, interest).
- _____ The mission of the group (service projects, evangelism, starting groups).
- _____ Personal encouragement.

Rank the following spiritual development needs in order of interest to you with 1 being the highest and 5 being the lowest:
- _____ Learning how to become a follower of Christ.
- _____ Gaining a basic understanding of the truths of the faith.
- _____ Improving my disciplines of devotion, prayer, reading Scripture.
- _____ Gaining a better knowledge of what is in the Bible.
- _____ Applying the truths of Scripture to my life.

Of the various studies listed below check the appropriate boxes to indicate:
P - if you would be interested in studying this for your **personal needs**
G - if you think it would be helpful for your **group**
F - if **friends** that are not in the group would come to a group studying this subject

Growing in Christ Series (7-week studies)	P	G	F
Keeping Your Cool: Dealing with Stress	❒	❒	❒
Personal Audit: Assessing Your life	❒	❒	❒
Seasons of Growth: Stages of Marriage	❒	❒	❒
Checking Your Moral Compass: Personal Morals	❒	❒	❒
Women of Faith (8 weeks)	❒	❒	❒
Men of Faith	❒	❒	❒
Being Single and the Spiritual Quest	❒	❒	❒

Foundations of the Faith (7-week studies)	P	G	F
Knowing Jesus	❏	❏	❏
Foundational Truths	❏	❏	❏
God and the Journey to Truth	❏	❏	❏
The Christian in the Postmodern World	❏	❏	❏

Fellowship Church Series (6-week studies)	P	G	F
Wired for Worship (worship as a lifestyle)	❏	❏	❏
X-Trials: Takin' Life to the X-treme (James)	❏	❏	❏
Virtuous Reality: The Relationships of David	❏	❏	❏
Praying for Keeps (life of prayer)	❏	❏	❏
Character Tour (developing godly character)	❏	❏	❏

Becoming a Disciple (7-week studies)	P	G	F
Discovering God's Will	❏	❏	❏
Time for a Checkup	❏	❏	❏
Learning to Love	❏	❏	❏
Making Great Kids	❏	❏	❏
Becoming Small-Group Leaders	❏	❏	❏

Understanding the Savior (13-week studies)	P	G	F
Jesus, the Early Years (Mark 1 – 8)	❏	❏	❏
Jesus, the Final Days (Mark 9 – 16)	❏	❏	❏
John: God in the Flesh (John 1 – 11)	❏	❏	❏
John: The Passion of the Son (John 12 – 21)	❏	❏	❏
The Life of Christ	❏	❏	❏
Sermon on the Mount: Jesus, the Teacher	❏	❏	❏
The Parables of Jesus	❏	❏	❏
The Miracles of Jesus	❏	❏	❏

The Message of Paul	P	G	F
Who We Really Are: Romans 1 – 7 (13 weeks)	❏	❏	❏
Being a Part of God's Plan: Romans 8 – 16 (13 weeks)	❏	❏	❏
Taking on Tough Issues: 1 Corinthians (13 weeks)	❏	❏	❏
Living by Grace: Galatians (13 weeks)	❏	❏	❏
Together in Christ: Ephesians (12 weeks)	❏	❏	❏
Running the Race: Philippians (7 weeks)	❏	❏	❏
Passing the Torch: 1 & 2 Timothy (13 weeks)	❏	❏	❏

Men of Purpose Series (13-week studies geared to men)	P	G	F
Overcoming Adversity: Insights into the Life of Joseph	❏	❏	❏
Fearless Leadership: Insights into the Life of Joshua	❏	❏	❏
Unwavering Tenacity: Insights into the Life of Elijah	❏	❏	❏
Shoulder to Shoulder: Insights into the Life of the Apostles	❏	❏	❏

Words of Faith

	P	G	F
The Church on Fire: Acts 1 – 14 (13 weeks)	❏	❏	❏
The Irrepressible Witness: Acts 15 – 28 (13 weeks)	❏	❏	❏
The True Messiah: Hebrews (13 weeks)	❏	❏	❏
Faith at Work: James (12 weeks)	❏	❏	❏
Staying the Course: 1 Peter (10 weeks)	❏	❏	❏
Walking in the Light: 1 John (11 weeks)	❏	❏	❏
The End of Time: Revelation 1 – 12 (13 weeks)	❏	❏	❏
The New Jerusalem: Revelation 13 – 22 (13 weeks)	❏	❏	❏

301 Bible Studies with Home Work Assignments (13-week studies)

	P	G	F
Life of Christ: Behold the Man	❏	❏	❏
Sermon on the Mount: Examining Your Life	❏	❏	❏
Parables: Virtual Reality	❏	❏	❏
Miracles: Signs and Wonders	❏	❏	❏
Ephesians: Our Riches in Christ	❏	❏	❏
Philippians: Joy under Stress	❏	❏	❏
James: Walking the Talk	❏	❏	❏
1 John: The Test of Faith	❏	❏	❏

Life Connections Series (*Unique series blends master-teacher larger group format with effective small-group encounters; 13-week studies*)

	P	G	F
Essential Truth: Knowing Christ Personally	❏	❏	❏
Vital Pursuits: Developing My Spiritual Life	❏	❏	❏
Authentic Relationships: Being Real in an Artificial World	❏	❏	❏
Unique Design: Connecting with the Christian Community	❏	❏	❏
Acts: Model for Today's Church	❏	❏	❏
Critical Decisions: Surviving in Today's World	❏	❏	❏
Colossians: Navigating Successfully Through Cultural Chaos	❏	❏	❏
Intentional Choices: Discovering Contentment in Stressful Times	❏	❏	❏
Unleashed Influence: Power of servant Leadership	❏	❏	❏

Felt Need Series (7-week studies)

	P	G	F
Stress Management: Finding the Balance	❏	❏	❏
12 Steps: The Path to Wholeness	❏	❏	❏
Divorce Recovery: Picking Up the Pieces	❏	❏	❏
Parenting Adolescents: Easing the Way to Adulthood	❏	❏	❏
Blended Families: Yours, Mine, Ours	❏	❏	❏
Healthy Relationships: Living Within Defined Boundaries	❏	❏	❏
Marriage Enrichment: Making a Good Marriage Better	❏	❏	❏

For the latest studies visit www.SerendipityHouse.com or call 1-800-525-9563.

Personal Notes

Personal Notes

Personal Notes